Prai

"The Busines ... ~~version~~ of profound
business wisdo... ~~wisn~~ I had read it years ago so that the
lessons would have guided me through my career. This
book is a blueprint for achieving success in business and,
more than that, in life, too. It couldn't have been better!"
– *Richard Serrins, President, Marketing Analysts, LLC – MAi*

"Tony Nuzzo continues to impress with his thoughtful
and common sense approach to business and life. Readers will delight in the practical overview of the fundamental concepts of business explained easily through
real life circumstances and experiences. I loved it!"
– *Megan Kelleher, Managing Partner, Vaksam, LLC*

"Tony Nuzzo's book is a very enjoyable read and I applaud
his common sense approach to addressing the issues facing
businesses today. I highly recommend it." – *Peter F. Mawn,
Founder and Managing Partner, Oakmont Partners, LLC*

"Tony Nuzzo's book is an easy-to-read assemblage of
interesting stories and vignettes that are full of insights
and observations about both business and life. There
are lessons in it worth remembering and reminding oneself about time and again." – *Howard Wolk,
Co-President, The Cross Country Group*

"The Business PACT is a well-written, thought provoking
read that provides value to all who are building or running a
business. Even more valuable is the model Tony Nuzzo creates, demonstrating how we can find nuggets of gold if we
remain open to the lessons that are present in the vignettes
of our own daily lives." – *Carol Hempfling Pratt, General Counsel, Federal Home Loan Bank of Boston*

The Business PACT™

The Business
PACT
™

Connecting Business Thinking
with Daily Living

Tony Nuzzo
Stevie Award Winner

ISBN: 1439284679
ISBN-13: 9781439284674

Library of Congress Control Number: 2011960034
CreateSpace, North Charleston, SC

Dedication

This book is dedicated to my wife, Julie, who has been my life mate and best friend for about forty years already. The lessons I have learned and recorded in this book have been developed over time through our life adventures together.

Table of Contents

Introduction

A person does not need a graduate degree to understand and practice the key processes of successful businesses.

This book is designed to simply demonstrate the extremely strong and ever-present connection between the daily activities of life and the business knowledge opportunities created by just living normally on a day-to-day basis.

I have been in my own businesses, and I have worked for both large and small companies. I have worked in several of the best known and largest corporations in the world, including running marketing areas in Procter & Gamble, Johnson & Johnson, and American Express, and, after changing careers, running or starting banks at Chemical Bank, Fidelity Investments, and Marsh & McLennan. I have also been the primary organizer of a bank, which I currently lead, First Commons Bank in Newton, Massachusetts. In 2010, I was named the Financial Services Executive of the Year by the American Business Awards.

Each of my professional experiences over the years has had a building effect upon my business and personal knowledge and perspective. So, I am now sharing my cumulative understandings on successful business processes with you in an interesting, memorable, and practical way. This book may be particularly useful as a guideline for small business owners and their employees. It can also become a benchmark for large company employees who make an effort to better understand process tasks that need to be performed but are not explained to them. Additionally, this book can help students develop better business thinking.

I began this book on July Fourth, Independence Day. I chose this day because my wife, Julie, and I had just begun our vacation and it only seemed right to choose this day to "free" my thoughts and put them on paper. Additionally, given my intense and almost 24/7 work schedule, I wanted to use vacation to begin the time-consuming task of writing a book.

Each chapter in this book is a vignette or "slice of life" from fifty days in July and August. Each vignette shows how a person can learn about business by just thinking about the activities of the day.

Each vignette is grouped into one of four business categories representing the four key processes of a successful business. The four sections are:

- Planning
- Analysis
- Communication
- Teamwork

When you put the first letter of the four sections together, the letters spell PACT. Thus, I have named this book and the process of success in business, *The Business PACT.*

I usually begin each vignette with a statement or explanation of fact. This fact is either integral to each story or it helps to set up each story. Sometimes these introductory facts required research on my part. The research was exciting and rewarding. I often learned more than I would have thought in advance. Although I do not overtly discuss this idea in the book, I believe there is great personal gain when we make conscious efforts to expand our minds on a daily basis.

I conclude each vignette with a concise consolidation of how it ties with one of the key processes in business. Sometimes, the point is obvious. Sometimes, the point is a surprise. Always, the point is relevant.

Some venues in this book reappear. This is because I have centered the book on my life. As you think about the processes in this book in your own way, the venues will center on you. In other words, it does not matter where we are or when we think about applying the learning from this book—whether July and August or January and February—the principles are solid on a day-by-day, year-round basis.

My wife, Julie, is the one prominent reappearing character in this book and in my life. Julie and I met in college when I was at Boston College and Julie was at Newton College of the Sacred Heart down the street.

After I received my MBA from Columbia Business School, we started our married years in Cincinnati. It was there that I began a career in packaged goods marketing with Procter & Gamble and Julie worked as a full-time middle school and high school Spanish teacher. We also lived in Boise, Denver, and East Brunswick, New Jersey. Our three children, Beth, Michael, and Cortney, were born at St. Peter's Hospital in New Brunswick, New Jersey. As a family of five, we lived in East Brunswick, Toronto, Salt Lake City, and Wellesley, Massachusetts, just west of Boston and where Julie and I have been for the last thirteen years. We also have a home in Brewster, Massachusetts, on Cape Cod.

As a result of those many family moves, I think Julie and I, as well as our children, gained incredible perspective on life, on different types of people, and on business. However, after multiple moves and then landing in the Boston area, we were all ready to plant our roots. We are fortunate that our three grown children now live in the Boston area, too. Additionally, we have one beautiful grandson nearby, Nate, from Beth and her husband, Adam, who have also given us a grand-dog, Franklin.

It is now time to begin.

PLANNING

Planning is critical to the success of a business. It takes time, effort, and, sometimes, outside assistance. Planning starts with a statement of a mission and continues with an approach to achieving that mission within a carefully examined competitive landscape.

The vignettes in this section provide easy reminders on the importance of planning and the rationale for planning. After you absorb the messages from these vignettes, everyday activities will become reminders to plan while helping to create a willingness to plan carefully.

Planning should be periodic—for example, annually. This type of time frame allows for the proper measurement of executed activities in support of a business. Planning and re-planning on a continuous basis is really not planning at all. It is reacting.

Plans are never finished documents or thoughts. They are meant to be adjusted as circumstances change over time, and, if needed, they can be modified on a moment's notice—especially in time of crisis.

The Boston Pops performed their annual July Fourth Fireworks Spectacular tonight in the Hatch Shell on the Esplanade along the Charles River in Boston. The concert was seen by a live audience of over a half million people, and several million more people watched on local and national television, as Julie and I did from our home in Brewster, Massachusetts. We love listening to and watching the Pops and have seen them live in concert several times. As usual, the Pops put on a terrific show tonight.

The Boston Pops were founded in 1885 by Henry Lee Higginson. Higginson's plan was to bring lighter concert music to the public than that presented by traditional orchestras. The Pops have delivered on this plan from the beginning and have delighted audiences to this day.

In 1930, Arthur Fiedler became the first American-born conductor of the Pops. During his fifty year tenure, the Pops became widely popular, and they reportedly sold more recordings than any other orchestra in the world. Thus, they began gaining a following that could support a national television broadcast such as the one tonight, now led by Keith Lockhart who began conducting the Pops in 1995.

Henry Lee Higginson was born in New York City and moved to Boston as a youngster; he eventually became a successful businessperson.

Higginson had a strong desire for music to be played perfectly and he believed his musicians needed to practice extensively to deliver the quality, light music that he envisioned. Therefore, I can comfortably conclude that practice, practice, practice must have been the orders of his time, and practice remains a strong work ethic of the Pops today.

Speaking of practice, can you imagine, there were over fifty thousand people who came out last night to watch the Pops practice at the Esplanade! A large crowd watches the Pops practice every year on July Third in preparation for their July Fourth Extravaganza, but last night's rehearsal may have been the most important in their history.

The legendary Lionel Richie, who has numerous Grammy Awards and American Music Awards to go along with his Oscar, was scheduled to perform with the Boston Pops tonight. However, at the last minute Richie's doctors prohibited him from performing due to an illness.

As a result of Richie's ailment, Martina McBride stepped in to help the Pops. She, like Richie, is a highly acclaimed singer and songwriter having won the Country Music Association's "Female Vocalist of the Year" award four times and the Academy of Country Music's

"Top Female Vocalist" award three times. She and the Pops had only about seventy-two hours of notice that they would be performing together. New orchestral arrangements needed to be written immediately and there was little time for the Pops or McBride to practice independently or together. Yet, practice they did, and the show was magnificent as usual.

Higginson's plan for the Pops has proven successful for over 125 years because he understood practice was a necessary component to ensure a quality performance. He thought through how his plan would need to be achieved. His story is a good reminder for us to think through our plans. Otherwise, plans may fail shortly after they are begun.

Chapter 2

**Cape Cod
Baseball Temps
& Contingency
Planning**

In July, the Cape Cod Baseball League is in full swing!
Tonight there was a very important Eastern Division
League game played between the visiting Brewster
Whitecaps and the home team, Orleans Firebirds. It was
an exciting game with well over two thousand people in
attendance, including me and Julie rooting for Brewster.
Interestingly, in a spirit that would excite even the most
casual of fans, many, if not most, Orleans spectators visit
the field early—around noon or earlier for a 7:00 p.m.
game—and place lawn chairs or blankets on the grass
around the field to secure a seat for the evening game.
There are no bleachers or permanent seats of any kind
at the Orleans field, and choice lawn space is hard to
get! By the end of the night, the Whitecaps won 8 to 1,
and they looked very strong in hitting and pitching.

The Cape Cod Baseball League was founded in
1885, and it is the premiere summer league for college
ballplayers from around the country. To demonstrate
this point, let's use the Brewster Whitecaps as an

example. There were twenty-nine active major league players last year who had once been in a Whitecaps uniform.

In fact, every time someone watches a Cape Cod League baseball game, there is an average of six future major leaguers on the field! ...and the games are free of charge! ...and so is the parking!

One relatively unknown fact about the Cape Cod League is that there are temporary players in the league. These players are necessary for several reasons. One reason is that some players who have been recruited to join the league may be delayed from joining at the start of the season because their teams are in the College World Series, which runs late into June. Additionally, some players may become injured, and others may sign major league contracts before the season begins or during the season.

These temps are an important part of the league's success and an important part of the league's sustainability. If a team lost too many players during a season, without a contingency plan, the team and the league would fail. This league plan is particularly successful because it represents a win-win-win situation. With this temp plan, the league wins with the continuation of quality games, the temps win with the opportunity to shine—and some have made the league's all-star team, and the fans win with continued enjoyment.

The Cape Cod League has demonstrated a well-thought-out contingency plan by using temps. Contingency plans are necessary to ensure a business does not fail due to serious problems that can be considered and solved in advance. These problems can relate to a loss of key players as in the Cape Cod League or in a small business for reasons such as a person's health. Additionally, problems can relate to a natural disaster that damages the economics of a region or a business as is possible in cases of hurricanes or earthquakes.

In sum, when planning, do not forget contingency planning.

Chapter 3 | **Captains Course & Singles**

Since the first two weeks of July represent vacation time for Julie and me, I had the opportunity to play golf this morning.

I played at The Captains Golf Course in Brewster, Massachusetts, on Cape Cod. The Captains Course has two eighteen-hole courses—the Port Course and the Starboard Course—and it is rated by Golf Digest Magazine in the first twenty-five of America's Best Public Courses.

I went to the course early in the morning as a single because Julie does not play golf. As a single, I usually get on the course as a replacement for someone who does not show. In many ways, I am like a temp in the Cape Cod Baseball League. I take whatever opportunity comes my way, and I try to make the most of it. Usually, I am put together with three people who had their fourth not show up due to a child's illness or a late night out. As a result, the conversation on the course for the day usually revolves around the three friends but, once in a while, I get to add to the conversation beyond the customary, "Nice hit" or "Fore!"

Well, an unusual occurrence took place today. For some strange reason, I was put into a golf group with two other singles. I have no idea how this happened since the course was booked all day, other than to think an entire foursome did not make it to the course. Nonetheless, it was an experience worth noting and discussing.

Each one of us, each one of the three singles, had a great time today. None of us felt any pressure on our game. We did not know each other. We sometimes took two shots at a time for practice. This was possible because we were a threesome—and not a foursome—and we were moving quickly through the course. So, we did not need to worry about holding up the group behind us. We learned about each other as the morning progressed, and we enjoyed each other's company.

We learned that we each were trying to improve our game. That was why we went to the course as singles. We each talked about playing with our friends, but by the end of the day, we were friends ourselves.

The first person to join me at the first tee was an Austrian who lives full time in New Jersey and part time on the Cape. His name is Peter. He is a medical device salesperson in his sixties, and he is married. His wife sometimes plays golf, and she is an accomplished artist. He belonged to a golf club in New Jersey through last year but gave it up because he has not been able to play enough golf. He loves The Captains Course and was playing because he needs the practice.

The second person to join me at the first tee was a thirty-something-year-old who also lives in New Jersey. His name is Howie. He is an investment banker with a firm in New York City. He usually has trouble pitching and putting, and that is why he usually loses to his good friend. His wife is an elementary school teacher, and she does not play golf. It is their first time on the Cape. He was playing The Captains Course to improve his pitching and putting to, eventually, beat his good friend.

Then, there I am, a community banker who is almost sixty and married, who lived in New Jersey but now lives in Wellesley, Massachusetts, with a Cape Cod home in Brewster, Massachusetts. It was my first time playing golf this year and I needed the practice before I played with my friends later this month.

It was clear that all three of us had the common thread of needing to practice. This is part of the reason why we sometimes hit multiple balls from the same spot or putted multiple times until we sank a putt.

We all encouraged each other and cheered our good shots. It was a great time for three strangers who came together and found, as the morning progressed, that we had a common bond of practice, and this resulted in enjoyment that we had not expected. It was relaxing, productive, and worth repeating.

When we finished the eighteenth hole, we did not really know what to say to each other. We had such a good time, I think the customary "Nice game" was not enough. Therefore, Peter made the first move and suggested we grab a beer before we left. I concurred. Howie joined us.

We had an enjoyable conversation, exchanged contact information, and said we would stay in touch and, maybe, even play again together…all this after one morning of golf! It almost sounds like we attended summer camp together!

It is clear from this morning that business mirrors life. Sometimes, the unexpected occurs in business, and it can be positive or negative. Assuming the event is positive, as it was this morning with the three singles, we need to recognize the event in progress and move boldly toward extending the good fortune as we did on the golf course today.

Chapter 4 | **Golf & My Dad, Part 1**

Due to my work schedule, I have not played much golf over the last several years. This is not a complaint but just a fact.

The Leo J. Martin Memorial Golf Course is a public eighteen-hole course in Weston, Massachusetts, about four miles from our house in Wellesley. I went over to the Leo J. Martin course this afternoon to hit some golf balls at the driving range and to practice some putting. This was in anticipation of playing in a golf outing tomorrow with some business associates.

I have only played golf once this year, and today was only the second day this year that I picked up a club. My lack of playing this year is compounded by the fact that I only played golf twice last year and only once the year before.

At tomorrow's golf outing, my friend from college is being honored for his adult contributions to his high school. There will be several people there with whom I have business associations, including my friend who is being honored.

I have not played golf on a business day since 1997 or 1998—about thirteen or fourteen years ago when we lived in Salt Lake City, Utah. We belonged to a golf club in Utah, but we do not in Massachusetts. I found time to enjoy the outdoors in Utah in both the summer with golf and in the winter with skiing. I worked just as hard as I do now, but the geographic climate and mountain west way of life places importance on outdoor activities. Here in the New York-to-Boston corridor, we seem to have a culture of work, work, and work some more. Therefore, I am excited about playing golf tomorrow and thought that I had to practice. Tomorrow's outing has been planned for several months.

I bought a bucket of about 110 balls and went to the driving range. There were seven to twenty people on the range while I was there. These people included a few other individuals, a father with three grammar-school children, a mom with her two adult sons, a young adult male and his girlfriend, a father and his young son, and a golf professional giving lessons. This collection of people should be of no surprise because it was Sunday afternoon.

As I began to hit my driver, I dubbed a couple of balls. I had lifted my head, a mistake that I did not make when I was playing often. Then, I hooked a couple of balls, a mistake that I did not make when I was playing often. Then, I thought of my dad who passed away about eight years ago after a seven-year bout with cancer.

My dad began teaching me the game of golf when I was twelve years old. He continued teaching me into my forties. He loved the game, knew it well, and played often. He was a great golf teacher, although he said that he had trouble following his own advice.

As I thought of my dad's golf teachings, I began to keep my head down, I began to swing out, and I adjusted the alignment of my feet before swinging. Then, almost like a miracle, I hit the balls long and straight—a golfer's delight.

It will be interesting to see how I play tomorrow because I now have a plan. I will be thinking of my dad and his teachings...and, whether it be in business or in life, it is always better to be prepared rather than to wing it.

Chapter 5 | **Golf & My Dad, Part 2**

Well, today, I played golf in a charity tournament honoring my friend from college. Three business associates and I played in a foursome at Haverhill Country Club, located about forty-five minutes north of Boston in Merrimack Valley. Haverhill Country Club is a well kept, challenging course with an abundance of hills and sloping greens.

I played about as well as I could have imagined in this best-ball tournament. According to the rules, after all four players take a shot, all four players take the next shot from the position of the best ball, and more often than not, I had the best ball in our group. It was thrilling for me to be playing as well as when I lived in Utah about thirteen or fourteen years ago, when I played frequently.

Early in the tournament, my consistency and accuracy of play earned me the respect of my colleagues. Even I was amazed at my play. It seems my practice round in Brewster a couple of weeks ago and my practice yesterday at the range paid off today…and we had fun! Importantly, I was able to think of my dad's instructions on the game of golf on every shot, which helped me to do very well.

Well, the rain came as we began to play the eleventh hole. In fact, rain may be too weak a term. It was pouring cats and dogs! The sky opened up and buckets were poured on us. It was unbelievable! We were drenched almost immediately, but we continued to play—and my cart mate and I were probably the only two people on the course without a roof on our cart. Our initial golf cart ran out of battery on the ninth hole, and we traded our traditional battery-powered cart with a roof for the only remaining cart, a sporty, gas-powered convertible.

Although it was raining very hard, there was no lightning to halt the tournament, and, if any group did not finish all eighteen holes, that group would not be eligible to win. We persisted through all eighteen holes because, given our high handicaps and how well we were playing, we thought we had a very good shot at winning the tournament.

Our determination to win was most clearly demonstrated on the seventeenth hole, which is the second-hardest hole on the course. This hole is a 419-yard par four with the front edge of a large lake about 290 yards down the fairway. The lake is about sixty yards across to the far edge, and it spans the entire width of the fairway. It is about another seventy yards from the far edge of the lake to the beginning of a very large green.

Our best drive on the seventeenth hole went about 180 yards right down the middle of the fairway in the pelting rain. It was one of our shorter best-ball drives of the day, but we were fortunate that we were even able to hold our clubs as we stood soaking wet from head to toe to play the game. As a result of our drive, we had to choose either to lay up to the front of the lake and take another shot to reach the green or attempt a monster shot that would cross the water in the air and potentially reach the green in the heavy rain.

Our first team member took a lay-up shot and placed the ball in front of the lake. Then, in the torrential downpour, the other three team members, recognizing that I was having a terrific day and that we were in the hunt to win the tournament, asked me to "go for it." To carry the lake, I would need to hit a wood over 170 yards in the air in what now seemed to be a tropical rainstorm. That shot would almost equal the distance of our drive. Earlier in the day and before the rain, this would not have been an issue whatsoever. However, large, heavy raindrops were being blasted from the sky in a rapid-fire, highly concentrated manner, creating a situation that pushed golf shots to the ground prematurely. Nonetheless, we were going to give it our all to try to win. Thus, even if we lost, we could feel that we gave it everything we had.

So, I stepped out of our golf cart convertible in the heavy rain to address the ball, which I planned to hit over the lake in almost hurricane-like rain in an attempt to win the tournament for our team. As I took a practice swing, I felt that I could do it. Then, I took another practice swing and felt that I would do it. Then, I hit the ball. It was a beautiful shot...long, straight, seemingly perfect...but it was pushed into the water by the rain about three feet short of land. We all couldn't believe that the ball did not carry the lake. Then, one of my associates said, "Use a mulligan and go again." All four of us had bought two mulligans each at the start of the tournament, which could be used on any shot. A mulligan is a do-over. I had not used my mulligans so I had two more shots to take if I wanted—and I wanted.

On my next shot, I hit the ball long, straight, seemingly perfect...but it was pushed into the water by the rain about three feet short of land. It seemed to be an identical shot with the first. We were all aghast at the ball not carrying the water. It did not seem right, but the raindrops were almost the size of small hailstones, and they were coming in streaming concentrations, causing the ball to slow and drop quickly.

On my last shot, I hit the ball long, straight, seemingly perfect...but it was pushed into the water by the rain about three feet short of land again. It seemed to be an identical shot with the first two, reflecting my wonderful day of golf with regard to both accuracy and consistency. However, we were all disappointed at the outcome. We thought that I could beat the weather, but the weather beat me.

We continued to finish the seventeenth hole and, then, the eighteenth hole. We were one of the absolutely crazy foursomes to have played the entire eighteen holes in the heavy rain without any apparent regard for dryness, warmth, or logic, but we had a great time.

We had gone for the monster shot on the seventeenth hole because we were trying to win.

Sometimes we win, and sometimes we don't. Today, we did not win the tournament, but we gave it our best efforts and were all happy with our finish in the tournament. For me, I was delighted with my golf for the day. I had a plan to think of my dad and his teachings as I played today, and it helped me. It is great when a plan comes together!

Chapter 6 | **Continuing Education
& Be All That You Can Be**

Continuing education usually refers to an enriching or new learning experience for adults. Adults can receive formal continuing education from a wide range of courses given at schools and universities, community organizations, or online. Some of this formal training can be voluntary and some can be required. Voluntary courses can be in learning new languages, movie appreciation, or even baseball coaching. Required courses are usually for professionals, including accountants, insurance agents, real estate agents, and stockbrokers, in order to remain licensed.

Adults can also receive informal continuing education. This can come in the form of reading books and having book clubs, drinking wine and having wine clubs, and watching football and playing Fantasy Football. Additionally, people can look at the activities of each day and reflect upon them to discover ideas and lessons that enhance our thinking and, thus, our business and our lives, as is demonstrated with this book.

Today, I began another round of formal continuing education in order to maintain my insurance license for life insurance products, accident and health insurance products, and variable annuities. Although I am no longer a practicing insurance agent, as I once was for a short period in my career, I appreciate the time and effort that it took me to become licensed and the life knowledge that this process created. Further, since the law allows me to remain licensed although I am no longer in the field, I have chosen to do so because it continues to enhance my learning.

I am required by the state of Massachusetts to have forty-five approved continuing education credits in every three-year period. There is a wide range of courses from which I can choose, and I usually try to broaden or deepen my knowledge by choosing courses in areas that are either not top-of-mind for me or of great importance to me. The easy route would be to choose courses only in areas of my greatest strengths so that I could complete the courses in the least amount of time and with the least amount of pain. However, would taking the easy route be enhancing my thinking or improving my quality of life? The answer is no. If I chose the easy route, I would only be limiting my knowledge and, if I were still an insurance agent, I would not be maximizing my ability to help clients.

Taking an easy route when it comes to learning is bad planning. It is cheating ourselves in the short term and inhibiting our ability to maximize our opportunities in the long term. The simplest way that I can express how planning should be in our daily thoughts is to reiterate the Army recruiting slogan: "Be all that you can be."

Chapter 7

The Cape Cod Rail Trail & The Bike Pump

The Cape Cod Rail Trail is a paved twenty-two-mile surface with a width that can easily accommodate bicycles going in both directions simultaneously. The trail is not only great for cyclists but for walkers and runners as well. There is even a shoulder on this trail that is unpaved and sometimes used for horseback riding. The trail runs through six towns around the elbow of the Cape. Starting in Dennis, the trail goes east and then north through Harwich, Brewster, Orleans, Eastham, and Wellfleet. The trail runs along ponds, forests, and marshes as well as through some town centers. The scenery along the trail is beautiful.

Julie and I occasionally like to ride our bikes on the bike trail. We usually ride from our home in Brewster, which is very close to the bike trail, to the Chocolate Sparrow in Orleans for a drink or a snack. This is about a fifteen-mile round trip ride.

Today, Julie and I took our first bike trip of this summer season. It was a shorter bike trip than usual given the rainy weather forecast and our firsthand observation that rain might soon be upon us.

Before we began our ride, I filled the air in our bikes' tires using a brand new stand-up bike pump with a PSI meter that I purchased about a week ago. Usually, on our first bike ride of the season, which often occurs in June, we stop along the bike trail to fill the air in our tires. This is because the tires lose air from being exposed to the changing climates of the seasons in the garage from autumn to winter to spring.

We delayed riding our bikes until mid July this year primarily because riding with low air is difficult, slow, and painful for me. Therefore, I procrastinated about taking our first ride this year.

As I repeatedly pulled up and pushed down on the pump in our garage before we left for our ride, I began to think how great it would have been to have gotten this pump years ago so I could have avoided the grinding ride to the nearest bike store at the start of each new spring season. I could have saved the aggravation and the soreness associated with that first bike ride each year. All I had to do was take the time to plan how to remedy my issue, which was to buy a pump, and I would have prevented my painful first ride of each season. In short, we should not procrastinate in planning to solve our problems. Procrastination can create bigger problems down the road—pun intended!

Chapter 8

**Bank of New York Mellon
& Interest Rates**

The media is reporting the 512-point drop in the Dow
Jones Industrial Average as the headline news of the day.
This drop of 4 percent or so in the Dow is representative
of an overall market drop and concern over people's
investments, retirement, and other financial planning
needs. However, hidden under the news of the stock
market is, I think, the "real" big news of the day, from
the Bank of New York Mellon Corporation.

Bank of New York Mellon Corporation was formed
in 2007 as the result of a merger between the Bank of
New York and Mellon Financial Corporation. The Bank
of New York was founded in 1784 by Alexander Ham-
ilton, who went on to become the first United States
Secretary of the Treasury and a member of George
Washington's first cabinet. Mellon Bank was founded
by Andrew Mellon, one of the wealthiest citizens in
America in the 1920s, and he, too, went on to become a
United States Secretary of the Treasury, first appointed
by Warren Harding, then by Calvin Coolidge, and then
by Herbert Hoover.

The Bank of New York Mellon Corporation is a global financial services company operating in thirty-six countries with almost fifty thousand employees. It is not a retail bank that you would find on a street corner, but it is largely an institution that has a custody business and an asset management business for both corporations and very wealthy individuals.

Today, the Bank of New York Mellon said that it was going to charge some customers for putting money on deposit in the bank. Yes, a negative interest rate was established! Although the bank would only charge an eighth of a percentage point to customers with $50 million or more, it was a start to negative interest rates.

The bank's rationale for charging negative interest was that too much money was leaving the stock, bond, and money markets and going to banks where there is no volatility and where deposits are insured by the FDIC. The flight from the markets is due to many recent economic and political factors that have caused investor uncertainty and, as a result, big money is going into big banks. These banks need to find ways to utilize these deposits in order to make money. In today's economic climate, utilizing this abundance of cash effectively is hard to do, and a negative interest rate is an early potential solution to this dilemma.

I think the Bank of New York Mellon's negative interest rate is a signal that a new financial-planning era has begun. That is, where will money be kept safe, and what can individuals and companies do to keep their money safe?

The answer to safe money-keeping may lie in FDIC-insured bank deposits in the United States. So, based on supply and demand, if there is a rush to FDIC-insured bank deposits, bank deposit rates should fall from their already extremely low levels—which are, for the most part, paying below one percent on most short-term deposits today. Rates could move to where there will be a charge for holding funds by banks, and the Bank of New York Mellon will have been just the first bank to set out on this path.

It is not often that we see such a clear sign that a fundamental change may be occurring in an industry that affects so many other industries and individuals. Although it is not at all clear if the Bank of New York Mellon's move today may start a major trend, consumers, corporations, and banks need to consider planning for such a possibility.

In short, we always need to be on the alert for possible fundamental shifts in a market landscape and plan for numerous possible outcomes. Sometimes these possible shifts are hard to recognize because there are other distracting or pressing issues of the day getting in the way, such as the large stock market drop today overshadowing the Bank of New York Mellon news. However, we always need to look for news within our industries and be ready to adjust our plans when new marketplace information is received.

Chapter 9 | **The Dow & Ownership**

The Dow Jones Industrial Average is the subject of headlines in the news media today, from newspapers and radio to television and the Internet. The Dow plunged another 634 points today.

Charles Henry Dow founded the Dow Jones Industrial Average. Dow was a journalist who lived in the second half of the nineteenth century, having been born in 1851. Dow was also the founder of *The Wall Street Journal*. He died in 1902 at the age of fifty-one.

The Dow Jones Industrial Average is named after both Dow and his statistician associate, Edward Jones.

The Dow Jones Industrial Average is an index of thirty large companies' stocks, which are publicly owned and well known. I have worked in three of these companies: American Express, Johnson & Johnson, and Procter & Gamble.

So, when the stock market closed down 634 points today, that means the index of thirty stocks went down.

The Dow Index is based on the price of each stock weighted in a manner to keep all the stocks on a level reporting plane. For example, this means stock splits do not skew the average of the Dow. A stock split occurs when a company divides a share of stock into multiple shares. For example, if shares of Procter & Gamble were selling for one hundred dollars and the company decided to provide each shareholder with two shares at fifty dollars each in place of one share for one hundred dollars, this would be a two-for-one split. Of course, there are three-for-one splits, four-for-one splits, etc. There are even reverse splits. However, splits do not affect the value of the Dow because they are weighted neutrally for mathematical purposes.

Additionally, not all of the stocks in the Dow are industrial companies as the name implies. When Charles Dow and Edward Jones worked on the Dow Jones Industrial Average, America was best represented by industrial companies as a proxy for its corporate strength. Now, with changes made over time, the Dow has a mixture of companies from multiple industries as representative of our nation's business prowess. For example, heavy equipment is represented with Cater-pillar, a company that probably would fit the original meaning of an industrial company. Oil is represented with Chevron; software with Microsoft; food and bever-age with Coca-Cola; banking with Bank of America; etc.

The Dow's performance is a composite of several fac-tors from individual company returns and the nation's economy to world political events and global terrorism.

When the Dow closed down 634 points today, on a theoretical basis, the proxy for American corporate strength was hurt; this translated to damages in the retirement accounts of millions of Americans. However, you need to determine for yourself if you are going to be in the stock market and, if so, whether you will be in the market for the short term or the long term. This is because your perspective on investments will affect your analysis of the situation.

So, what is a short term and what is a long term? I personally think a ten-year time horizon is a long term. Therefore, anything short of this period I consider short term. However, some others, such as those who are younger or have more tolerance for risk, may consider the long term twenty years or thirty years.

So, after hearing the news of the stock market drop today, I decided to look at how stocks performed over the last ten years—my long term. In round numbers, the Dow has moved from about 10,300 in August of 2001 to about 10,800 in August of 2011, a slight increase.

I also decided to look at how gold and silver performed over the last ten years. In round numbers, gold moved from about $270 per ounce in August of 2001 to over about $1,700 per ounce today—up over 500 percent. Silver moved from about $4 per ounce to almost $40 per ounce—up almost one thousand percent.

I now need to consider whether I want to do additional analysis on whether I should buy gold or silver, which I do not currently own, or own fewer or no stocks, or choose yet a different course of action. I also need to decide if I would like the help of a financial advisor. I need to look at the stocks in my portfolio and my 401(k) and decide if any should be sold or increased in shares, and there are a myriad of other factors that I could consider if I want to adjust my current investment plan. However, in the end, despite all the analysis that can be performed, my investment results are just that— my results reflecting my plan.

Planning in business is also complex, with multiple variables. Analyses on subjects can be performed almost indefinitely. However, at some point, you need to decide when you are confident to move forward with a plan. Too much analysis may prevent action. However, in the end, remember, you own your plan—someone else does not.

Chapter 10 | **The Dow & Facing Facts**

The Dow plunged another 520 points today. Again, we have explosive headlines. People are frozen rather than thinking and planning for themselves. Newscasters and journalists are feeding the frenzy of concern. The only advice I have heard on the news tonight is, "Sit tight and do not open your monthly retirement account statements this month." The newscasters are referring to the investment principle of buy and hold, a core principle in investment planning.

The buy and hold theory refers to putting money into quality stocks or mutual funds and holding on to that investment for the long-term rather than getting involved in daily trading, despite any volatility that may occur. The reason for this teaching is the belief that, over the long term, the stock market goes up and a solid return will result. The theory continues that average investors are busy at their homes or at their work and do not have the time or expertise of professionals to know when to buy and sell on a regular basis.

The stock market has basically stayed even over the last ten years. So, why buy and hold stocks for the long-term? Is the long-term longer than ten years for some?

Should alternative investments like gold and silver be considered? Should I try to time the market? Should I place more money in a bank? Should I sit tight because I am happy with my investment plan? This is a complex set of planning issues for which relevant, up-to-date information is needed—including that which is contained in my monthly retirement account statement. Otherwise, I cannot plan—even if my current plan is to sit tight, or do nothing.

In business, a person cannot be afraid to face facts. Otherwise, wrong plans and decisions can be made. A person cannot hide his or her head in the sand as some newscasters have recommended to general audiences today by saying, "Do not open your retirement account statements this month because it will be too painful." In short, a plan is not a plan if there is not a sound basis for it with a regular monitoring process that would allow revisions to a plan that goes off course.

Chapter 11

Seventy-Year-Old Man & His Medicare Selection

I recently completed a continuing education course on Medicare as part of my desire to maintain my life insurance, health and accident insurance, and variable annuities licenses. For me, Medicare remains a very complex subject to study, despite having studied it in the past. Yet, it does not seem complex to everyone. Somehow, virtually everyone who has worked ten or more years and is sixty-five years old or older needs to make a choice about Medicare coverage, and some people who are disabled or have special kidney issues are eligible for Medicare, too. Therefore, thousands of people make decisions about Medicare every day without complaining or feeling the complexity of the program as I do.

Briefly, Medicare provides basic health care benefits to Social Security recipients. Those who are not eligible for Social Security can receive Medicare benefits by paying a monthly premium. Otherwise, Medicaid is available.

Medicare is funded by the Social Security Administration with a budget roughly equal to about 10 percent of the entire US budget, and it is currently available to about 40 million people. Medicare is in four parts and broadly speaking:

- Medicare Part A is hospital insurance.
- Medicare Part B covers the services of doctors and outpatient care. It also covers some preventive services like flu shots. Part B requires a premium payment every month.
- Medicare Part C is Medicare Advantage, a series of programs provided by private insurance companies for supplemental coverage with different monthly premium costs, different co-pays, and different annual deductibles.
- Medicare Part D covers prescription drug costs.

Of course, there are enough rules and nuances in Medicare to fill books, but the general idea is above.

Today, Julie and I reached the Cape in time for me to run to the hardware store to buy some replacement bulbs for the recessed lights in our Brewster kitchen.

When I arrived at the hardware store, a man with a bandage on the right side of his forehead asked if he could help me.

I asked the man, "What happened?" He said that he had just had some skin cancer removed, but he was going to be okay. He also said that he was seventy years old and had good Medicare Advantage coverage. So, he was able to afford the cancer removal.

He said he was fortunate with his selection of a Medicare Advantage plan. The person he met with in the Social Security office at the time of his Medicare selection took the time to walk him through his Medicare options, and he made a good Medicare Advantage pick on the spot. However, when he walked into the Medicare office, he volunteered that he really did not know anything about making a Medicare Advantage selection.

As this seventy-year-old man directed me to the proper aisle, I was happy that his Medicare Advantage plan seemed to be working for him. He relied solely on the input of one Social Security representative for information on Medicare at the time of his selection. He trusted a stranger, within a period of a half hour or so, to guide him in making a critical medical decision that will affect the remainder of his life.

Leaving your fate to others is not planning. Although a subject may be complicated, taking the time to carefully analyze alternatives before making a decision is prudent in any field. Otherwise, we are just gambling. For example, what would have happened to the seventy-year-old man if he had met with a Social Security worker who inadvertently guided him in the wrong direction with his lifetime medical selection?

Chapter 12

The Young Married Couple & Driving

Utah has a population of almost three million people within about eighty-five thousand square miles. This results in a population density of about thirty-five people per square mile. Utah contains a large portion of the Wasatch mountain range and several beautiful national parks, like Zion National Park near the Arizona border.

Salt Lake City is the capital of Utah, and it has almost two hundred thousand people in its metropolitan area. Salt Lake City is a beautiful city located in the Salt Lake Valley, which is an area stretching from Ogden, about forty miles north of Salt Lake, to Provo, about forty miles south of Salt Lake. The Wasatch mountain range is on both the east side and the west side of the valley. These mountains are very steep and tall and hold snow all year round at their peaks. Snowbird is one of the more famous skiing areas around Salt Lake, and it is located only about thirty minutes southeast from the heart of the city. The peaks at Snowbird hold snow all year long; Snowbird keeps its ski lifts open all year round so, if you want, you can ride up the mountain and play in the snow in the summer while wearing only shorts and t-shirts! We, as a family, lived in Salt Lake City for about six years during the 1990s, and we thoroughly enjoyed the climate and the outdoor way of life.

Montana has a population of about nine hundred thousand people within about one hundred forty-five thousand square miles—the size of an area slightly larger than Japan and almost 75 percent larger than Utah. This results in Montana having a population density of about seven people per square mile. Montana contains mountains and national parks, too, like Glacier National Park near the Canadian border.

Massachusetts has a population of about six and one half million people within about seven thousand eight hundred square miles. This results in a population density of about eight hundred and thirty-three people per square mile. We, as a family, have been living in Massachusetts for about thirteen years and, as you can tell from the writings in this book, it is a great place to live, offering everything from sports to the Cape and more. However, the population density of the state as a whole is, remarkably, over twenty times the density of Utah and over one hundred times the density of Montana.

We had the twenty-five-year-old son of some of our Utah friends come to visit with us today, along with his twenty-five-year-old wife of two years, who is from Montana. This young couple now lives in Salt Lake City, and they are about to take eight months off from school to do volunteer work at a Christian mission in an impoverished city in India. Upon returning to the

United States, the young man will begin his residency at a hospital on his way to becoming a doctor, and the young woman will begin her pursuit of her PhD in Public Health. They plan to stay with us for a couple of days as they look at hospitals and schools in the Boston area as possible considerations for places where they will resume their studies after their return from India.

The young man called Julie today at about eleven o'clock and said, "We are about to leave our initial stop along the east coast, Washington, D.C., and we hope to be at your house by dinner." This is because the young couple looked at their directions and saw that the trip from Washington, D.C., to our house in Wellesley in the Boston area was only about 430 miles away; in the states of Utah and Montana, traveling 430 miles on open highway at ninety miles per hour is a breeze. The young couple thought the trip would only take four to five hours at "mountain" travel speed. Julie just said to the young man that they should not plan on being here for dinner, as previously expected, because "the drive will take longer than you think, drive safely, and please call us along the way."

The young man called Julie again at about five o'clock from near Newark, New Jersey, and said to Julie that traffic was unbelievable—it was nothing like Utah! He also wondered, "How close are we to your house?" Julie informed him that he was still about four hours away under good driving circumstances. So, she said they should eat some food, drive safely, and call us if they needed some additional perspective.

Ultimately, the young couple arrived at our house well after nine o'clock, or about ten hours after they began what they thought would be a relatively short and easy drive. To their credit, they called for perspective on the drive at the time of their departure and along the way. However, if they had thought about calling us for perspective the night before they left, they may have left Washington, D.C., before 11:00 a.m. in order to make their dinner plans; Julie had prepared a wonderful meal for them. However, they had not yet adjusted their own perspectives from a mountain west view to an east coast reality with a population density twenty to a hundred times that of Utah and Montana, respectively.

Coincidentally, our son and his girlfriend stopped at our house after the young man from Utah and his bride from Montana called at five o'clock. We invited Michael and his girlfriend to join us for dinner, and we had a great feast and a good time. Although this feast was planned for the young couple from the mountain west, it was put to good use with Michael and his girlfriend.

Julie did have late evening food for our visitors, and Michael and his girlfriend stayed at our house until shortly after the Utah couple arrived. Michael and the young man knew each other in Utah because our families are good friends. During the evening, all of us laughed about Michael and his girlfriend eating the meal prepared for our Utah guests, and we caught up on Utah news. As a result, Michael and the young man, who were planning to get together tomorrow night anyway, had an early and fun start to their visit.

Planning is seldom easy when done properly. For this young married couple, the distance on a map had to be considered in combination with population density. They missed the population density overlay as they began their trip from Washington, D.C., to Wellesley. Understanding the environment in which a plan would be executed is critical for its success, as this young married couple found out today. This includes a thorough knowledge of the competitive landscape as well as any reasonable obstacles that can be conceived.

Chapter 13 | **The Young Married Couple & The North End**

The North End of Boston is one of the oldest sections of the city, founded in the 1630s. The North End today has a large population of residents who are either from Italy or have Italian roots. There are numerous restaurants, bakeries, gelato stores, and shops. There are also festivals each weekend in August with vendors of all types—from those offering pasta or sausage to those offering jewelry or t-shirts. Additionally, these festivals have carnival-type game booths and bands of musicians weaving themselves through the narrow streets filled with people and vendors. The bands usually play uplifting songs, adding to the fun atmosphere. To top it off, our daughter, Cortney, lives in the North End, allowing us to visit the area frequently!

Julie and I took the young married couple from Utah to the North End this afternoon. They had never seen anything like the street celebration that they witnessed today. For example, three bands with about a dozen or so musicians each actually squeezed past us on various closed side streets with vendor booths on both sides and crowds of people in the middle. It seemed everyone was purchasing food or products from the booths. We had a fun time, and there was much energy in the air. We even went to one of our favorite restaurants in the North End, Pagliuca's, for dinner and, as is customary in the North End, we went to a favorite bakery for dessert.

As we were finishing dessert, Cortney, who had a scheduling conflict so she was unable to meet us for dinner, joined us at the bakery to see our guests. The couple told Cortney they were happy to see her and they were excited about being in Boston. They were now ready to begin serious consideration of Boston as the next place to pursue their studies. Within this context, the young couple began asking questions about the cost of living in Boston. They asked about the cost of apartments for the short term and the cost of houses for the long term.

After Cortney left, Julie and I proceeded to spend much time during the balance of the day discussing the cost of housing in Boston and in other northeast cities. In short, this couple was somewhat shocked at the cost of housing in the northeast as compared to the mountain west states of Utah and Montana, in particular.

This couple may go "all in" financially over the near term and go to school in the northeast after they complete their Christian missionary work in India. However, it may be more financially prudent in the near term for them to continue their academic and medical pursuits in the middle or southern part of the country. However, they are considering the long term benefits of continuing their education in the northeast—both academically and financially. In the end, they are attempting to weigh all the factors in their lives before they make a choice for learning continuation, and these factors include instructors, peers, and housing costs in the near term and work environment, living environment, and housing costs in the long term. This is a good demonstration of comprehensive planning with consideration given to time frames. A plan needs a time frame to be effective, and we should remember to consider all the relevant factors. Sometime, if we forget some factors, it won't matter. Sometimes, it will. All the time, we should give a planning exercise our best efforts.

ANALYSIS

Analysis is critical to the success of a business. Careful analysis guides and supports a plan by creating measureable benchmarks for the plan, thereby validating or invalidating the planning process over time. Like planning, it takes time, effort, and, sometimes, outside assistance. An analysis is usually presented using tables or charts or spreadsheets. Business progress according to a plan should be analyzed, at least monthly, to determine whether any tactical changes to a business need to be made to keep the business on or ahead of the plan.

Analysis is critical to all decision making. Whether decisions are made instantaneously or sequenced over time, rational decisions are based on clearly defined thought. Irrational decisions are made without the benefit of analysis, and irrational decisions can lead to the demise of a business.

The vignettes in this section provide memorable reminders to think through decisions. Of course, hardly anyone ever admits to making an irrational decision, but many businesses have failed over time. In fact, statistics show that a majority of new businesses fail within the first five years. My working assumption, based on my own observations, is that most of the people associated with business failures did not apply either the *planning process or the analysis process, or both, to the development of a business or the ongoing activities of a business. I also assume many current businesses have not been optimized for the same reasons.*

Chapter 14

Bramble Inn & Hail Mary

Julie and I went out for dinner tonight with two other couples at the well-known and highly rated Bramble Inn in Brewster. The dinner represented the third annual Cape Cod dinner together for the six of us during the first two weeks of July. Each couple lives quite a distance from the others, but all of us have close ties with each other. We had hoped to complete our dinner in an hour and a half because one person, who for privacy purposes I'll call John, has late-stage cancer in one of his vital organs. He has lost a significant amount of weight and tires quickly. We did complete the dinner in an hour and a half, but then the real conversation began, and it continued for at least another hour and a half.

What do I mean by real conversation? Well, no one wanted to address John's cancer. We knew that we were fortunate that he made it out to dinner and, due to that fact, everyone kept the conversation upbeat and general during dinner. For example, we spoke about families, children, grandchildren, current events, and the like. However, at the end of dinner, we thought that it might be nice to get together again next week. Then, all of a sudden, John said he might not be around next week. There was dead silence. Then, I asked, "What do you mean?" John said they might be in Florida. I said, "Why?" He said that they might go for some one-of-a-kind cancer treatment being developed in Florida. He and Jane (another made-up name for privacy purposes) have been researching this treatment for a couple of weeks, and they think they may go. Well, now the real conversation began.

We were all extremely interested in knowing more about John and Jane's possible trip to Florida next week, especially since John was scheduled to begin chemotherapy next week in Boston. We desired an explanation for this one-of-a-kind treatment, and we hoped to know whether the Florida treatment would replace the scheduled chemo or be used in addition to the chemo. Basically, since John was very close to each of us, we all began to open up with our feelings; two other people at dinner had been diagnosed with cancer within the last two years. Needless to say, the conversation became very personal as the three people out of six who have experienced cancer spoke about their firsthand experiences.

It became clear to me tonight during our dinner conversation that John and Jane were diagramming a "Hail Mary" play—which is not just used in football. In football, a Hail Mary play is when a quarterback throws a long pass into the end zone to one or more receivers without any time left in the game in an attempt to score a touchdown and win the game on the last play.

John and Jane analyzed John's situation and determined that a successful Hail Mary play is needed to keep John in the game of life. They determined that, if they did not call a Hail Mary play, John—continuing with a football analogy—would just be "running out the clock," or conceding his fate.

Due to analysis, John and Jane determined that they were going to search for every possible remedy to John's disease. They were not going to give up.

Sometimes in business it is easy to give up—especially when the situation looks dire. However, I have found that businesses that succeed have "fight" in them...and there is nothing wrong with analyzing a situation and calling a Hail Mary play, if needed. Sometimes they work, but more often they do not. Yet, I believe, they are always worth the effort.

Chapter 15

Nauset Beach & "Look At Me!"

Nauset Beach in East Orleans, Massachusetts, is a beautiful beach that is part of the Cape Cod National Seashore. The Cape Cod National Seashore was established in 1961 when President John F. Kennedy signed a bill to preserve and protect parts of New England. The Seashore includes a forty-mile stretch of continuous beach that includes Nauset Beach. I sometimes see or read that beaches on the National Seashore are among the most highly rated in the world.

At one point at Nauset Beach today, Julie and I were standing at the edge of the water with our feet in moist sand that became covered with salt water with each incoming wave. A grandmother and a small boy passed in front of us, moving from north to south. The boy must have been about two years old, and he was carrying a beach ball about the size of a basketball. Just as he passed Julie and me, he stopped in the water of a remnant wave and yelled, "Look at me!" Then, he reiterated in his loudest voice for all who did not pay attention the first time, "Look at me!"

This young boy was very proud that he was standing in the ocean, and he wanted to the world to see him.

Upon seeing this young boy's excitement and hearing his exhortation, I said to myself, "Look at me!" What does the world see? What do I see?

Businesses must be introspective, too. Knowing and analyzing strengths and weaknesses are integral to success. Misdiagnosing internal competencies could lead to competitive vulnerabilities and, ultimately, a demise of the business. Much time and thought need to be given to an honest introspective analysis of a business in order to help ensure success. Just remember the exciting and thrilling voice of a two-year-old who said today, "Look at me!"

Chapter 16 | **Pilgrim Monument & Relevance**

The Pilgrim Monument is in Provincetown, Massachusetts, which is at the outermost tip of Cape Cod. The monument memorializes the pilgrims who made their first landing on this continent in Provincetown in 1620. Five weeks after landing the Mayflower with 102 passengers, the pilgrims moved on to Plymouth, Massachusetts. Importantly, the Mayflower Compact, which outlined the principles of civil and religious liberty and the practices of a genuine democracy for this country, was not signed in Plymouth, but in Provincetown Harbor.

Julie and I took a fifty-minute ride to Provincetown today to revisit the Pilgrim Monument and enjoy the day in this town, which has miles of high rolling sand dunes and a distinctive village of activity and commerce.

During the last few years, we have visited Provincetown once per summer and focused our day on one specific activity. For example, last year, we enjoyed a boat trip into the open sea around the tip of the Cape to watch whales, and we had the rare privilege of viewing three species of whales on one trip: humpback whales, minke whales, and fin whales. It was an incredible whale watch, and we had not taken a whale watch in several years.

Today, we enjoyed the Pilgrim Monument, which we had also not visited in several years, and we began to put the height of it into perspective with other national monuments. For example, the Pilgrim Monument is 252 feet tall, or a little taller than Bunker Hill Monument in Charlestown near Boston, and about half the height of the Washington Monument.

Interestingly, the Pilgrim Monument is the tallest all-granite structure in the United States. It has 116 steps and 60 ramps to get to the observation deck. Today, Julie and I climbed every step, walked every ramp, and enjoyed the views from each side of the tall, rectangular building. From one perspective, we were even able to look across Cape Cod Bay to Brewster, where we have our Cape home.

Speaking of Brewster, we also learned from the monument's museum literature that the Town of Brewster has been singled out on a historical basis for creating the momentum for building the Pilgrim Monument in the early 1900s. As best I can deduce, this may have been due to the passion of the descendents of William Brewster, who was on the Mayflower and was a signer of the Mayflower Compact.

I enjoy history, and I found today's return trip to the Pilgrim Monument fascinating. It made me think about school and what I learned about the Pilgrims' landing in America.

I believe I was taught in school that the Pilgrims landed in Plymouth, Massachusetts. As a result, we have the famous Plymouth Rock, in case anyone doubts this fact. I also believe that it is a popular belief that the Pilgrims landed at Plymouth Rock and, then, formed Plymouth Colony.

I do not remember ever being taught that the Pilgrims landed in Provincetown before they landed at Plymouth Rock. I asked Julie if she remembered what she was taught regarding the Pilgrims landing in America. She said that she remembered the same set of facts that I did—the Pilgrims landed at Plymouth Rock, and there was no mention of Provincetown.

The Mayflower landings at Provincetown and at Plymouth Rock were less than four hundred years ago. Yet, we cannot seem to keep the correct educational perspective on the dual landings in our history books or in our classrooms or in our popular beliefs.

History is easy to distort over time...and so are business facts and information. We must analyze facts as they become known and move forward based on the best available data. In the case of the Pilgrim Monument and history today, it is not as important or relevant in today's society to know the exact Pilgrim landing place as it is to know the principles brought to this continent by the Pilgrims. However, in business, it may not always be so easy to gloss over mistakes. Analyze facts and information carefully and continuously for both relevance and accuracy...and, as interesting as non-relevant information may be, do not waste time distracted from key issues.

Chapter 17

**Air Conditioning
& Business Models**

Willis Haviland Carrier invented modern air conditioning in 1902, and he later formed The Carrier Air Conditioning Company—today's world leader in air conditioners. Cleverly, movie theatres were among the first purchasers of air conditioning units in order to attract large crowds during the hot summer months. Folklore has it that the Folies Bergere Theatre in New York City installed the first air-conditioning system in a theatre in 1911. The Packard Motor Car Company was among the first auto companies to offer air conditioning as an option in the 1930s. Window air conditioners for homes began to become popular in the 1950s. Now, air conditioning is commonplace and, sometimes, taken for granted.

Today, Julie and I left Brewster because vacation was over. However, before we left to return home, Julie and I met with two different air conditioning repair people regarding a modification to our central air conditioning unit in Brewster. One person came to the house at 10:00 a.m., and one came at noon.

The first air conditioning person, who is the owner of his business, gave us an estimate for the unit's modification on the spot and a timeframe for performing the necessary work. The job would take one day, but the work could not start until after Labor Day, even though he knew we wanted the job completed before the start of August. He also knew we were securing multiple bids. He said that he did not have sufficient staff to do the work earlier than Labor Day. He said that he runs his business so that he keeps an even workflow throughout the year for him and his employees.

The second person, who is also the owner of his business, gave us an estimate for the work on the spot and said that he hired extra help in the summer to accommodate the summer influx of part-time residents. He said the work would take one day, and he could start in a week—which meant he could have the job completed before the start of August as we requested. The price for his work was the same as the first person's. He knew we were securing multiple bids.

Both owners told us that our request for air conditioning work was right in the heart of their busy summer season. Yet, both traveled about thirty minutes to examine our system on a busy summer Friday on the Cape. Each person told us that people decide they need work on their air conditioning systems when the weather is hot. This theory is supported by the fact that little or no air conditioning work is performed by these companies in December! Nonetheless, the comparison between these two well-known and respected owners of firms with regard to having them perform work for us is stark.

The owner of the first company tries to maintain steady work for his crew throughout the year—air conditioning work in the summer and heating work in the winter. He is comfortable and busy with his approach to the business. He does not need to worry about not having sufficient work to pay all his employees.

The owner of the second firm gears up in the summer in anticipation of the influx of part-time residents on the Cape by hiring part-time contractors. His business is booming, and each year he has significantly increased sales and profits. He does not worry about having sufficient work to pay his full-time employees on a year-round basis because much of the summer work is accomplished with seasonal workers who are happy with their roles.

Each owner has a valid approach to his business model. However, one firm can grow, and the other has chosen not to grow.

In other words, a business is what a person makes of it. Hiring part-time contractors and attempting to grow his business is extra work for the owner of the second firm compared to the owner of the first firm. However, the owner of the second firm analyzed his business and his life, and the rewards of using part-time contractors outweigh the extra work. These rewards could be in community recognition of his business expertise and growth as well as financial gains. The first person has no need for extra work, recognition, or increased financial gains.

It is important to analyze your business model for appropriateness and competitiveness from both a short term and a long term perspective. For example, not only did the second owner get our business today, but he will get our future business, too. The first owner may think he has a steady flow of work all year round, but that work could dry up if his competitiveness is not increased. Therefore, analyze your business and change your model, if necessary. Seek assistance from accountants, lawyers, and consultants with this approach because introspective analysis is a difficult and complex task.

Chapter 18

PET Scans & Vince Lombardi

A PET scan is unique body imaging; the name PET is short for positron emission tomography.

We often hear of PET scans with cancer patients because a PET scan can identify abnormal tissues or organs in the body, like cancer cells or tumors.

A PET scan requires a person to have radioactive tracer fluid injected into an arm, lie down on a flat examination table, and be moved into a doughnut-shaped machine that reads the tracer fluid and converts images into three-dimensional pictures. This tracer fluid contains glucose or sugar. The scan takes about forty-five minutes.

A three-dimensional PET scan picture is created when different types of tissues in the body absorb different levels of the glucose-filled tracer fluid and, as a result, reflect different degrees of brightness. Normal tissue uses glucose for energy. This normal tissue absorbs a baseline of tracer fluid, which is reflected as a dark color in pictures. Cancer tissue uses more glucose than normal tissue. The cancer tissue absorbs more tracer fluid than normal cells, which is reflected as a bright color in pictures.

I returned to work today after vacation concluded, and Julie and I received two big pieces of cancer news.

First, John, who had dinner with us at the Cape two weeks ago, received the results of his PET scan. We thought he had late-stage cancer in one of his vital organs, and there was hope that a "Hail Mary" play could keep him in the game for a while. Unfortunately, the PET scan revealed that the late-stage cancer in one organ had spread to other parts of his body. It was devastating news for everyone who was privy to this information. This means that John and Jane may not be able to call a Hail Mary medical play, even if they wanted, because doctors may feel John is past the point of potentially life-saving medical treatment.

Second, my cousin Gerry called and said that his younger sister's husband was in the hospital again as part of his six-year battle with cancer. In fact, he had gone "code blue" three times in the last week or so. "Code blue" is used in hospitals to indicate that a patient needs immediate resuscitation.

Gerry and his wife, Rose, live in Florida, and they had just traveled to Connecticut for two weeks to vacation with family, including visiting with Gerry's younger sister and her family.

Gerry now seems to think the "game" may be rapidly approaching a finish for his younger sister's husband; this was very difficult news to absorb, especially after hearing John's news.

So, here we have two people who are, apparently, near the end of their lives. What happens when a business is nearing the end of its life? There are many options that need to be analyzed. Is it past the point of possibly being sold? Are there any valuable assets remaining? Are there any liabilities, like bank loans? As you ponder these questions and others, it is fitting to think introspectively of yourself in a manner that is best captured in a quote from the late, great Green Bay Packers football coach, Vince Lombardi, who said, "It's not whether you get knocked down, it's whether you get up." Lombardi's quote is relevant in many aspects of business today.

Chapter 19 | **Entrepreneurs &
Tartufo Restaurant**

An entrepreneur is a person who has a new venture or idea or, even, a dream. This person becomes accountable for the development and eventual results of that venture, idea, or dream. Frankly, I consider myself an entrepreneur.

The word entrepreneur came from an economist who was born in Ireland in the 1680s and later moved to France, where he gained French citizenship. His name was Richard Cantillon.

Cantillon divided workers into two groups: fixed-income earners and non-fixed-income earners. Entrepreneurs are non-fixed-income earners because they are unsure of their income-producing value. This value is based on whether or not they correctly predict consumer preferences with the development and execution of their ideas.

Dante Bellucci is co-owner of Tartufo Restaurant in Newton Centre, Massachusetts. His business is an Italian restaurant with outstanding food, a terrific ambiance, and fair prices. His restaurant is within fifty yards of where I work, and I have conducted most of my business lunches and dinners at his restaurant. We have become friends over the years.

Dante's business was closed today for renovations. Dante started this restaurant seven years ago, and he thought that he needed to change the menu, ambience, and prices this year, despite his success. He has been working on this renovation for several months, but the actual construction only began around the beginning of this month, and he hopes to have the project completed by the end of the month. Since summer is slow for business in Newton because many people are at the Cape or elsewhere, he thought now was the best time of the year to do the renovations.

I bumped into Dante on the sidewalk between our buildings, and he invited me over to his restaurant for a tour of the construction in progress. The hardwood floors were installed on the first floor already, a new stair railing to the second floor was in place next to a new seating station area, the bar was significantly lengthened and awaiting new granite, and the area behind the bar was entirely new and a different color than the old one—now with mirrors and mini pillars. The restaurant was a work in progress, but I could tell that it was going to look terrific when completed; Dante was very proud.

Dante, as a very experienced chef and restaurant owner, also spoke with me about his philosophy that a restaurant needs to update or change its look every seven years. He said it creates "buzz" and excitement that carries a business to new heights. Therefore, as he did the physical change to his restaurant, he would also make a different menu to be more in tune with the times from a health perspective and a price perspective. I questioned him again, as I have done in the past, about why he would want to tamper with his success. He answered confidently, as he had in the past, that he analyzed his business and he is doing what is best for his customers.

Dante is living the description of Cantillon's definition of an entrepreneur. He is predicting consumer preferences and, since he is a non-fixed-income earner, he is betting his livelihood that he is right.

Entrepreneurs take risks every day based on analysis—sometimes using instantaneous analysis and sometimes using more carefully thought-through analysis. Regardless of the analysis you use, like Dante, you should know your customers.

Chapter 20 | **The Jukebox & Land Ho!**

In 1973, a jukebox was a coin-operated, metal box-like device that usually hung on a wall or was mounted on tabletops in an eatery or bar that allowed patrons to pay for selected songs chosen from records enclosed and played in the box.

Today, Julie and I had lunch at Land Ho! in Orleans, and we had a twenty-minute conversation with the owner of the restaurant, John Murphy, whom we have known for decades.

John Murphy started his Orleans restaurant and bar in 1969 and now has additional restaurants in Harwich, Massachusetts, a nearby town on Cape Cod, and in Costa Rica. He has the best clam chowder on Cape Cod.

I asked John when he started having live music in his restaurant on weekend nights. This is because Julie and I, along with our son, Michael, and his girlfriend, experienced his live music in Harwich on Friday night, and Julie and I had experienced his live music in Orleans last year. John said the live music was the idea of his three grown sons and he only agreed to it in recent years. He then proceeded to tell us a story about how much he opposed live music in the past.

John told us that a bandleader came to Land Ho! to speak to the owner one night in 1973. This bandleader could not find the owner at first because there were too many people crowded into the establishment talking, drinking, eating, and generally having a good time. After a while, the bandleader approached John and asked, "Are you the owner?" John said yes. The bandleader said that John should hire his band because he could really make the place "hop." Then, John thought to himself that his place couldn't "hop" anymore than it was already. There was a packed, lively crowd in the restaurant, and he was already out of room for additional people.

John decided to answer the bandleader's request to play at Land Ho! in the following manner. He pointed to the jukebox on the wall and said that is where he gets the music for his restaurant. The jukebox doesn't eat, it doesn't smoke, it doesn't complain, and it pays him five hundred dollars per week. If the bandleader wants to play in the restaurant, there would be no free food, no smoking, no complaining, and the band would need to pay him five hundred dollars per week. Needless to say, the bandleader decided not to play at Land Ho! ...and John's quick analysis demonstrated his clarity of thought and deep understanding of his business. Enough said.

Chapter 21 | Time Flies & Plutonium-Powered DeLorean

What is time?

This question has been asked through the ages. Time can be used to set meetings in business or school or anywhere. In this way, time is linear; time brings order out of chaos. Time can be used to determine how long meetings last or how long someone lives. In this way, time measures duration, and time allows planning and history to occur. Time can be used to determine how fast someone runs a mile or how long a football game is played. In this way, time allows champions to be born.

Some have argued that time is a singular dimension through which events flow. Taken to an extreme, this theory would, theoretically, allow for time travel. Time travel postulates that, with the proper molecular speed, one can travel either forward or backward in time. Time travel was depicted in the 1985 comedy movie, *Back to the Future*, starring Michael J. Fox as Marty McFly. Fox's character took off in a plutonium-powered DeLorean car and met his teenage parents-to-be before they were ever married. He needed to ensure that other time travel-related events did not cause his parents to separate as teenagers, never marry, and never have him as their son.

This singular dimension theory of time through which events flow has a serious side as well. For example, Sir Isaac Newton, the famous English mathematician, physicist, and astronomer of the late 1600s and early 1700s, is a subscriber to this theory.

Others have argued that time is an intellectual invention of convenience for comparing events; events do not flow through time. Each action in the universe is singularly catalogued and passes away with the "sands of time," never to be seen again. Additionally, since time does not contain events, it cannot be traveled—either in comedy movies or in life. Immanuel Kant, the famous German philosopher of the 1700s and early 1800s who wrote extensively on experiential thinking, is a subscriber to this theory.

There are some aspects of time that are indisputable by either the people who think along the lines of Newton or the people who think along the lines of Kant. Specifically, seasons change.

Well, Julie and I were finishing dinner at our house in Brewster tonight when we noticed how very dark it was outside at 8:30 p.m. This was the first time this summer that we were shocked by the upcoming change of the season—especially since we were still in July. It gave me pause to think about how fast the seasons change and how little time we have left this summer to do all that we want to do. In essence, time flies. This is a truism that needs to be kept top of mind in business. There is never enough time to accomplish all that is needed, so tasks need to be analyzed and prioritized to maximize the mission of the business. Without analysis and prioritization of tasks, time will fly and the business will be left behind...and there will not be a plutonium-powered DeLorean waiting to take you back to the future to correct the situation.

Chapter 22

**Pan-Mass Challenge
& Connecting The Dots**

The Pan-Mass Challenge is an annual weekend series of bike rides by individuals to raise money for cancer research and treatment at the Dana-Farber Cancer Institute, which is located in Boston. The Pan-Mass Challenge was the country's first fundraising bike-a-thon, founded in 1980. Since then, it has raised over $300 million for cancer research.

The Pan-Mass Challenge was this weekend, and two of the eleven routes of the weekend extended through the entire length of the Cape, from the beginning of the Cape in Bourne to the tip of the Cape in Provincetown. There were thousands of cyclists on these two routes today, and many thousands of additional friends and family members came to the Cape to watch the riders. The riders, in general, completed their rides between 8:30 a.m. to 2:30 p.m.

Julie and I left Brewster to return to Wellesley around 2:00 p.m. today. We thought that we would have a quick ride because an early afternoon time for departure from the Cape is usually traffic free. The traffic usually builds later in the afternoon after people have had their last few minutes on the beach or shopping.

It usually takes forty minutes for Julie and me to travel by car from Brewster to the Sagamore Bridge via Route 6. So, today when we drove up the ramp to Route 6, we were shocked to be joining a backup of vehicles that were all headed for the bridge. I got off of Route 6 a couple of times to try backup routes, but nothing worked. We eventually kept returning to Route 6 and, in total, it took us about three hours to reach the Sagamore Bridge—a direct route of only twenty-seven miles to get off the Cape. This translates to a speed of only nine miles per hour; the Pan-Mass cyclists traveled at a faster pace than this.

All we had to do to avoid this traffic nightmare getting off the Cape today was to think about the Pan-Mass Challenge. We support riders in the Pan-Mass Challenge every year, including this year. We knew the Cape rides took place today. It was all over the news on TV and in the newspapers. All we had to do was connect the dots.

In business, it is sometimes very easy to miss the obvious due to day-to-day pressures. However, we must continually analyze our surroundings in order to prevent a possible, unexpected setback that could have easily been avoided. Just remember to connect the dots.

Chapter 23 | **Cheesesteaks & Originals**

A Philadelphia cheesesteak has thinly sliced sautéed beef and melted cheese in a long roll or a hoagie. The sandwich can have American, Provolone, or some other type of cheese, and, when cooked in combination with the beef, the sandwich produces a tasty juice that usually drips from the roll when eaten. Toppings can be added to the sandwich, like onions, mushrooms, ketchup, and peppers.

It is said that the Philadelphia cheesesteak was first made in the 1930s by a South Philadelphia hot dog vendor named Pat Olivieri. Olivieri put some beef on his hot dog grill for himself, and a taxi cab driver noticed the aroma and asked for his own steak sandwich. The next day, according to the legend, cabbies from around the city came for steak sandwiches. Soon after that, Olivieri opened up his own store and added cheese to the steak in his sandwiches.

Today, I walked to lunch at Linden Deli in Wellesley. The Linden Deli is a landmark establishment in the town and noted for great sandwiches of all types. It is not a very big store. There are only about a dozen seats at the counter and another dozen or so stools at an island in the middle of the store. I was fortunate to find a seat at the counter today. I ordered a specialty sandwich, but the person next to me ordered a cheesesteak.

I found the occasion to strike up some casual conversation with the person sitting next to me eating the cheesesteak. He said that he had traveled to Philadelphia often and had hundreds of cheesesteaks, but this Linden Deli cheesesteak was the best of all. He proceeded to laud the sandwich and expand upon his rationale, having established himself as a cheesesteak aficionado.

I thought to myself about the rationality or irrationality of comparing the Linden Deli cheesesteak with a genuine Philadelphia cheesesteak. We always want to compare ourselves or our items to an original. However, why do we not logically think that a copy can be better than an original?

In business, there is nothing wrong with analyzing the practices of other companies and implementing the best practices in your own company. Further, best practices should be improved in order to advance your company versus the competition. Just because someone had an original idea or practice, it doesn't mean that the original is the best.

Chapter 24 | **Steve Jobs & Clear Thought**

Steve Jobs stepped down from his CEO post at Apple this evening. Although he gave no reason for his resignation, it is widely assumed that his failing health is the primary reason.

There will be much said about Steve Jobs in the media and, I think, it should all be good. He is legendary. Briefly, he and fellow Apple founder, Steve Wozniack, started Apple in Jobs' parents' garage. Over time, the board of Apple ousted him from his own company. Yet, years later, he was asked to return to Apple to lead the company against its adversary in the marketplace—Microsoft, which was led by co-founder, Bill Gates. Jobs returned to Apple without any appearance of holding a grudge against the people who had previously fired him.

Today, thanks largely to Steve Jobs, Apple is one of the most valued companies in the world as measured by Stock Market Capitalization. That measure is calculated by taking the number of shares in the company sold in the market and multiplying that number times the price per share. In fact, there has been a day or two this summer when Apple finished a stock-trading day in the number one worldwide position for valuation—ahead of such giants as ExxonMobil, IBM, and, of course, Microsoft. With his company, Steve Jobs has created tens of thousands of jobs and, more importantly, changed the lives of everyone on this planet by inventing products such as the Mac, iPhone, and iPad.

I read Steve Jobs' resignation letter to his board tonight. In his letter, and I paraphrase, he indicated that if he ever felt that he could not perform his duties to the fullest satisfaction of himself, he would tell the board and he would resign. In other words, he would not need the board to tell him that he was no longer needed or wanted.

Steve Jobs' resignation letter provided me with a deep insight into the man. With his letter, he summed up the principles of self-awareness and dispassionate analytical thought. He seemed to have practiced these same principles when he returned to the company after having been previously fired. He used clear-thinking analysis at both times. His thought was not encumbered by emotion. He probably used this same type of analytical thinking in Apple on a day-to-day basis as well.

In business, clear, rational thought is needed. Often, emotions cloud our thinking. Steve Jobs is a reminder to us to stay focused on issues and not miss achieving goals due to thickheadedness or emotions.

COMMUNICATION

Communication is critical to the success of a business. Planning sets direction. Analysis provides credibility to and measurement of a course of action. Communication lets others know what you want to do, how you want to do it, why you want to do it, when you want to do it, who should do it, and how much it costs. Communication takes time to do right, and often outside assistance is required to help shape a message.

Communication is used in every aspect of a business, in all forms of marketing from advertising to selling, and in all forms of operations from purchasing to producing. It is used in all media from television and radio to billboard and the Internet. It is used within a company with employees and potential employees and outside a company with customers and vendors. Communication affects the actions and desires of others. It provides us with the opportunity to delight our customers and keep them coming back. Miscommunication or inappropriate communication can undercut a mission, product, service, or customer base. It can also hurt business partners and employees. Words and other types of contacts need to be carefully chosen and presented in the proper tone to maximize effectiveness.

The vignettes in this section are impactful messages to remind you of the importance of carefully crafted communications.

Chapter 25

**Fourteen-Year-Old
Spanish Boy & English**

Seymour Pond is a 181-acre natural kettlehole pond
on Cape Cod with an average depth of twenty feet and
a maximum depth of thirty-eight feet. In other words,
Seymour Pond is really a good-size lake with its northern half in Brewster, Massachusetts, and its southern
half in Harwich, Massachusetts. It has over two miles
of shoreline with more than a dozen species of fish,
including yellow perch, white perch, smallmouth bass,
and largemouth bass. Of note, kettlehole ponds are
shallow, freshwater bodies of water on the Cape that
were formed by glaciers on their way back toward the
North Pole.

Our Cape Cod home is in a Brewster community
with an association of residents who have a private beach
onto Seymour Pond. Having private access to a beautiful pond is wonderful. This is because ponds are great
for swimming after going to the Bay or to the ocean and
for canoeing, kayaking, and fishing. They are great fun,
as are the lakes in Maine, for example.

Well, Julie and I were at our beach on Seymour Pond
late this afternoon and, as on most hot Saturdays in July,

about two dozen people were there, with an about-even split between adults and children.

Julie and I were sitting on the dock in the pond when a fourteen-year-old boy paddled up to us on his tube. He looked at me for a minute and asked me in a noticeable Hispanic accent, "Where are you from?" I said I was from Boston, since this is easier to explain than Wellesley for someone who does not know Massachusetts' towns. Then, I asked the boy, "Where are you from?" He said clearly, "Spain."

Since my wife is a former high school Spanish teacher, I asked her to ask the boy a few questions in Spanish, like, "Where in Spain do you live? Who are you visiting here? Do you know what baseball is?"

To my delight and Julie's, this fourteen-year-old boy asked Julie to speak to him in English.

We learned much about the boy in a few minutes. For example, he is an exchange student staying with a family in Vermont, and the mother in that Vermont family has her mother in our Seymour Pond community. However, most importantly, we learned that this boy is intent on learning English and the American way. He told us that he already tried kayaking today, which Julie and I observed. He wants to go to a beach on the ocean next, and he wants to learn about baseball. He said his Vermont family is very nice, but he misses his sister in Spain. We asked him about whether he played football—our soccer—but he would only address the sport as soccer since he was in America.

This fourteen-year-old boy wanted to learn our language and culture, and he wanted to eventually communicate with Julie and me at an equal level.

The boy understood that effective language communication would allow the free flow of ideas between people without any barriers or possible miscommunications caused by translations or cultural misunderstandings. He wanted to create a level playing field for himself.

In business, you should make every effort to deliver a message in a manner that can be easily understood by the person receiving the message. Understanding the language and the culture of the party receiving your communications is a good first step. Effective message communication provides a clear and honest transmittal of facts which maximizes business impact and minimizes unanticipated problems. Overall, good communication will enhance business productivity.

Julie and I had another gorgeous day at Nauset Beach today in Orleans. We had a perfect July day. Temperatures were in the nineties with bright sunshine. There was a clear blue sky all day. The waves were manageable and the surf was clear. Additionally, hundreds of beach umbrellas formed a vision of bright color dots against the golden sand, which added to an uplifting feeling of enjoyment.

At one point during the day, eight young girls parked their chairs and towels to my left as I looked at the water. In other words, they were slightly north of me, but within clear earshot, only being six or so feet away and facing me due to the position of the sun to the south and their desire to get tan.

Based on hearing the conversation of these girls, which I could not avoid if I wanted, these girls seemed to range in age from having just completed freshman year of high school to having just completed sophomore year of college, and some of the girls seemed to be sisters.

The girls talked about everything from music to school. The most animated part of the conversation for these girls seemed be around school. They were discussing each grade through their current time in college. Although not everyone had gotten to college yet, everyone had completed grammar school. Within this context, the conversation began to revolve around the "best grade ever."

Interestingly, a couple of the younger girls said the sixth grade was the best grade ever. Then, the oldest girl said the sixth grade was the best grade ever because it was a high learning year combined with the beginning of freedom.

The conversation became chatter filled, and everyone talked about how great the sixth grade was. They even remembered their teachers and many of their assignments. There seemed to be unanimity of thought around the sixth grade being a breakout year for learning and freedom, and for having great teachers. Then, I began to think of my own sixth grade experience.

I began sixth grade in New Haven, Connecticut, where I was born. Then, in December, my family moved to Park Ridge, New Jersey. So, I had two teachers in sixth grade, and I cannot remember the name of either one.

I only have one clear memory from sixth grade. That memory is from my first day of school in New Jersey, after the December break. I began to play in the asphalt school yard at lunchtime with some other students. We were playing some kind of ball game. As we began to play, one student, his name was Richie, called me Tony. At first, I did not know who Richie was calling. I had never been called Tony before that moment. I was always Anthony—and that is how I was introduced to the class that morning. However, Richie was one of the smartest students in the class; he was the first to "figure out" that my nickname was Tony, and he used it.

I have been called Tony ever since that lunchtime break on my first day in the school yard of my New Jersey grammar school.

I think of how different the name Tony feels to me than Anthony. I also think of how different the name Tony is to others versus Anthony. As a result, I believe my life would have been different if I had gone through life as Anthony versus Tony. To better explain my feelings here, I am going to use Kate Middleton as an example. She married Prince William. Her given first name is Catherine. I wonder if she would have become a princess if she had been called Cathy, Cath, Kitty, or Kat.

In business, selecting words, including names, is very important to communication. Words convey images and tones. The proper words can shorten communications while enhancing understanding. Improper words may need clarification and, as a result, time may be lost and misunderstanding may occur. You should give words significant thought before using them. That is what I remember from sixth grade. What a year!

Chapter 27 | **Japanese Visitors & Sharks**

The current Chatham Lighthouse was built in 1877. Chatham is on the elbow of the Cape Cod, and it has always faced rough seas with strong currents and dangerous shoals, or sandbars. Lighthouses were built early in our nation's history along the outer beaches of Cape Cod to help guide ships safely through these perilous waters. At one time, there were about twenty working lighthouses on Cape Cod; now many are no longer active. The Chatham Lighthouse was the second lighthouse built; Highland Lighthouse in Truro was the first. One of the most beautiful beaches on Cape Cod is directly across from the Chatham Lighthouse. It is called, simply enough, Lighthouse Beach.

Today was a cool day on the Cape, and Julie and I decided to go to Chatham. As part of our visit, we drove about half a mile off the main street with shops to Lighthouse Beach. We looked out at the beach from an elevated parking area between the beach and the lighthouse. We gazed at the beauty of the semi-circular beach, along with dozens of other people, and we also noticed that no one was in the water.

Lighthouse Beach was closed due to shark sightings. Over the last few years, unfortunately, this has not been an uncommon occurrence at this beach. This is because the seals on the Cape have been protected, and they are overpopulated. Sharks swim up from the warm waters south of Florida just to feast on these plump creatures during the summers.

At one point today, we were looking at the beach next to a group of six or seven summer visitors from Japan. The Japanese visitors seemed to be enjoying the beauty of the beach and the seals in the distance. I was clearly able to discern from these visitors—who were not speaking English at the time—that this beach visit had been a planned stop on their itinerary. However, I was also able to understand from their gestures and excitement that they really wanted to see a shark. They were pointing toward the water in different spots and getting anxious about something; I think they wanted to see a shark before they had to proceed to their next tourist spot. Of note, there were hundreds of people looking at the beach and the water while we were there today; I think everyone hoped to see a shark. In that respect, these Japanese visitors were no different than those from New York, New Jersey, Connecticut, Quebec, or elsewhere.

The Japanese did not need to speak English for me to understand what they were thinking and doing.

In business, words do not always need to be spoken and papers do not always need to be written to communicate effectively. Sometimes the most effective communications are nonverbal or unwritten. However, the key to this type of communication is not making a mistake on the interpretation of the nonverbal signal. With the Japanese visitors, who were not speaking English at the time we stood next to them, it was easy to determine their intent—especially when hundreds of people around them had the same idea! However, nonverbal communications are not always so clear. There may be a need for clarification. Clarify, if necessary. Mistakes can be costly.

Today, Julie and I took our fourteen-month-old grand-child, Nate, to the Warren School Park in Wellesley to play. As part of our time at the park, we enjoyed watching Nate play in the sandbox. There were toys in the sandbox ranging from a two-foot-long plastic shovel truck to a beach bucket with shovels. There was also one other child playing in the sandbox at the time, Owen. The sandbox is about twelve feet by twelve feet with a one-foot-high wooden wall around it, which is especially helpful for adults like me who want to sit and play or guide, when appropriate.

Nate does not yet use words, but he is very good at grunting and pointing. He also seems to clearly understand the words we speak to him. Owen was older than Nate, but he did not speak much.

Nate and Owen were able to share toys politely and easily. They both were frustrated when they were unable to effectively communicate with each other, but they never grabbed toys from each other.

There is a commonplace expression that asks something like, "Why can't everyone play in the sandbox together nicely?" This saying applies to adults who have trouble getting along. However, it usually implies a major, tangible issue is occurring. It does not usually imply a communication issue like the one I witnessed today.

I think the folklore around both children and adults having trouble playing in a sandbox is wrong. Fighting over toys as a tangible issue did not occur in the sandbox; I am not sure that is the major issue for adults who cannot get along. There was a failure to communicate today, which caused the problem in the sandbox—plain and simple.

In business, people must recognize when there is a failure to communicate, and a failure to communicate should not be masked in some other type of created issue that distracts from the root problem. If communication is not occurring clearly and easily, people become frustrated, and it may not be worth the effort to continue "banging away" at the subject. There are too many other things to do.

Chapter 29 | **Cancer Stats & Delivering A Message**

The American Cancer Society is a nationwide, community-based, voluntary health organization dedicated to eliminating and preventing cancer. It was formed in 1913 by fifteen physicians and businesspeople in New York City.

According to the American Cancer Society, currently, men have a one in two chance of developing cancer over a lifetime, and women have a one in three chance. These are astronomically high odds to me. To compound matters, men have a one in four chance of dying from cancer, and women have a one in five chance.

My cousin, Gerry, and his wife, Rose, drove up from Connecticut to meet with Julie and me for lunch today. We had not seen Gerry and Rose since my mother passed away about three months ago. Halfway through lunch, Gerry received a call from his daughter informing him that his sister's husband had just died. This news takes away an appetite.

It seems to me that the American Cancer Society has a problem with communication that is demonstrated in many types of messaging. Specifically, if men have a one in two chance of developing cancer, and women have a one in three chance, why haven't we found a cure? Is no one listening?

Clearly, if every American knew and understood the odds of getting cancer, there would be an all-out, concentrated effort to rid the world of this disease. Yet, cancer is battled in dispersed research centers, companies, universities, hospitals, government agencies, and other like centers. There is no central command center to battle cancer, and information is often shared only through industry journals. To me, this is a seemingly ineffective process with a time lag, and to a cancer patient, time may be costly.

I think Americans think there is a strong effort to find a cure for cancer, and it is nice to either donate to one's favorite charity in this area or to think that someone is donating. However, nice does not work here because chances of developing cancer are so high. Think about what would happen if one in two males and one in three females were to be injured by a terrorist attack during their lifetimes. I think we would have serious, concentrated efforts by this country to prevent this occurrence. Yet, we do not have that with the cancer battle. Why? The odds and impact of cancer have not been received or absorbed by the general population.

In business, delivering a message and having it absorbed are two different things. How often have you heard the saying, "That just went right over my head?" Messages must be delivered in easy-to-comprehend language in a memorable and impactful form. For example, just think how differently our society might battle cancer if someone began a message with, "Look to your left and look to your right. One of those two people will get cancer..." A message is not a communication if it is not understood.

Chapter 30

Flash Mobs & New Media

Legend has it that flash mobs began in 2003 due to the efforts of a *Harper's Magazine* editor named Bill Wasik. He was able to get over one hundred people to go to Macy's in New York City to surround a rug at an appointed time. Then, he was able to get two hundred people to go to the Hyatt Hotel and begin fifteen seconds of applause at the communicated time.

Today, there are reports of flash mobs in Philadelphia and in London. These mobs are not applauding. They are looting and causing all sorts of trouble. Some news reports indicate that the flash mob participants are having fun causing damage. Leaders in Philadelphia and in London have said, in effect, that there is a breakdown of morals in our respective societies that is causing these problems.

Of course, the flash mobs in Philadelphia and London are reprehensible. However, they are loosely organized due to new media tools: Facebook, Twitter, and other social media outlets. These tools were also recently used to help organize opposition to governments around the world; some governments toppled due to opposition supported with new media communications.

New forms of communication need to be studied at their inception. It may not always be easy to see the uses for these new forms of communication in the beginning. However, as time progresses and uses become clear and applicable to business, new media should be adopted and enhanced where applicable. It is imperative in business to find the most effective and efficient forms of communication to maximize business results.

Chapter 31

**Mr. Potato Head
& Customer Delight**

Charlestown is a neighborhood of Boston located north of downtown Boston on a peninsula. Charlestown was originally a separate town from Boston and was the first capital of the Massachusetts Bay Colony. The territory of Charlestown originally included what is now Melrose, Malden, Somerville, Winchester, Everett, Woburn, Burlington, and parts of Stoneham and Wilmington. Charlestown became a city in 1847. Residents of both Charlestown and Boston voted that Boston should annex Charlestown in 1874.

Charlestown is well known for being the site of the Battle of Bunker Hill on June 17, 1775, its influx of Irish immigrants in the 1860s, and its massive gentrification process in the 1980s. Today, with its proximity to downtown Boston and its colonial, row-house homes, Charlestown is a vibrant community that includes young professionals who have an easy commute to Boston. Our oldest child, Beth, her husband, Adam, our fourteen-month-old grandson, Nate, and our granddog, Franklin, live in Charlestown.

On most Wednesdays, I drive Julie to Charlestown in the early morning and pick her up when I finish work. This is because Julie takes care of Nate on Wednesdays; giving Julie a ride back and forth gives me an opportunity to spend a few minutes with Nate before he goes to bed.

This Wednesday, Julie brought Nate a Mr. Potato Head. Mr. Potato Head was invented by George Lerner. According to legend, Lerner had the idea for this toy when he put body parts on vegetables that he took from his mother's garden to create dolls for his younger sisters. Lerner sold an early version of his toy to a cereal company and, later, the company that eventually became Hasbro bought the rights to the toy. In 1952, Mr. Potato Head became the first toy advertised directly to children, rather than parents, on television, demonstrating that we should all know how to best target and communicate our business products and services for maximum results.

When I entered Nate's house tonight, Nate wanted me to see Mr. Potato Head. Although he does not yet speak words, he is very smart. When I asked him, "Where is Mr. Potato Head's mouth?" Nate pointed to Mr. Potato Head's mouth. When I asked him, "Where are Mr. Potato Head's ears?" Nate pointed to Mr. Potato Head's ears. When I asked him, "Where is Mr. Potato Head's baseball hat?" Nate pointed to Mr. Potato Head's hat, took it off, put it on his own head, and started to laugh. Then, of course, Julie and I laughed, too. It was great fun, and probably the reason Mr. Potato Head continues to be a popular toy to this day.

In business, we need clear communications. Nate demonstrated this tonight when, in response to my direct questions about Mr. Potato Head, Nate pointed to the direct answer on Mr. Potato Head. Nate did not nuance the answer or ask me to define a verb before providing a response. He did not even use words. My questions were straightforward, and Nate's answers were straightforward. Communication was simple, yet complete. In fact, it was enjoyable; we even laughed. Communication in business would be much more enjoyable with a similarly straightforward manner. Just think of customers who yearn for direct, honest answers from many companies. Straightforward communication is the first step toward delighting customers. The rest depends upon the answer, of course!

Negotiation:

BusinessDictionary.com defines negotiation as: Bargaining (give and take) process between two or more parties (each with its own aims, needs, and viewpoints) seeking to discover common ground and reach an agreement to settle a matter of mutual concern or resolve a conflict.

Wikipedia defines negotiation as: A dialogue between two or more people or parties, intended to reach an understanding, resolve point of difference, or gain advantage in outcome of dialogue, to produce an agreement upon courses of action, to bargain for individual or collective advantage, to craft outcomes to satisfy various interests of two persons/parties involved in negotiation process. Negotiation is a process where each party involved in negotiation tries to gain an advantage for themselves by the end of the process. Negotiation is intended to aim at compromise.

The Free Online Dictionary defines negotiation as: A discussion set up or intended to produce a settlement or agreement.

Entrepreneur.com defines negotiation as: The act of discussing an issue between two or more parties with competing interests with an aim of coming to an agreement.

Barron's Business Dictionary defines negotiation as: The process of bargaining that precedes an agreement.

I think you now get the idea of the meaning of negotiation.

Julie and I returned to Brewster tonight so that our central air conditioning system can be modified tomorrow. The work will begin at 8:15 a.m., and it should be completed by the end of the day.

On the car ride to the Cape, we listened to the radio—AM, FM, and Sirius. The news of the day continued to be on the negotiations in Washington regarding raising the national debt ceiling. Apparently, there continues to be no progress on an agreement to raise the debt ceiling, and the August 2 deadline is rapidly approaching.

The news calls the talks in Washington regarding raising the debt ceiling a negotiation between parties. I think this is wrong.

The Washington discussions on the debt ceiling do not meet the definition of negotiation. There does not seem to be a matter of mutual concern (according to BusinessDictionary.com). There do not seem to be parties intending to reach an understanding (Wikipedia). There do not seem to be parties intending to reach a settlement (The Free Online Dictionary). There does not seem to be an aim of coming to an agreement (Entrepreneur.com). There does not seem to be bargaining that would precede an agreement (Barron's Business Dictionary).

The recently completed labor discussions between the National Football League (NFL) players and owners stand in sharp contrast to the Washington discussions on the debt ceiling. I think this contrast provides proof that the Washington discussion on the debt ceiling is not a negotiation.

The NFL owners and the NFL players have their livelihoods on the line with their negotiations. For them to proverbially feed their families, they need to perform work; football is what both parties do. Therefore, football is needed for both parties. As a result, it is no wonder there was a settlement in time to keep the regular season on its original schedule. There were common economic interests shared by the owners and the players.

In the Washington discussions on the debt ceiling, there are no economic interests shared by the president, the senators, and the house members on this issue. For example, it is unlikely that any lawmaker will be seriously affected by possible rising interest rates due to a possible downgrade in the country's credit rating if an agreement is not reached. Further, a lack of an agreement, in itself, will not affect any lawmaker's income, unlike the NFL owners and players. The lawmakers—from the president to the house members—will still be working if an agreement is not reached by the deadline.

The common interests shared by the president, the senators, and the house members relate to getting reelected. Reelection causes an extension of their incomes and their power. One vote on one matter will not, in itself, usually cause any president, senator, or house member to lose a position along with its associated income and power. Therefore, the whole debt discussion by our national lawmakers is about reelection, not about solving the problem.

In business, it is critically important to understand when there is "skin in the game" and when there is not "skin in the game." A person with little or no vested interest in a solution is not likely to straightforwardly address issues and problems and move toward a solution. When possible, always try to negotiate with the person who has the most "skin in the game," or be ready to waste your time with your communications. You may be strung along almost indefinitely until the person without a vested interest finds an angle of personal benefit to assist with resolution, and the angle may not necessarily relate to the business problem being solved.

East Boston is a neighborhood of Boston that has long served as an initial home for new arrivals to America. It has most recently welcomed a growing Latino population and many Italians have grown roots in the community from a previous generation of immigrants. There are about forty thousand residents in this neighborhood.

Rino's Place is an Italian restaurant located in a residential area of East Boston. You would never think there was a restaurant in its location, except for the fact that people are always milling around the residential-looking white building. Only upon close examination can a person determine that the crowd is not of concern, but one that is waiting to get in for some incredible food at reasonable prices.

Rino's has been around nearly a quarter of a century, and it has a wait for dinner every night. Only parties of six or more can make reservations, and there are a very limited number of reservations accepted in any given month. We had made a reservation for six for tonight months ago.

Julie and I took our son, Michael, his girlfriend, and our daughter, Cortney, to dinner at Rino's for Michael's thirtieth birthday celebration tonight. Another of our son's friends was scheduled to come but couldn't make it at the last minute. Therefore, I offered to pay for an extra meal when we took our seats, but the head person in the dining room said that was not necessary. I thought that was very gracious—especially at 8:00 p.m. with a large crowd still waiting outside.

It was the first time at Rino's for Julie, Cortney, and me. Our son and his girlfriend manage to get in periodically, but Julie and I have never decided to wait for a table in this small restaurant with forty or so seats. Yet, we know it has an outstanding reputation for freshly made pasta, large portions, and all sorts of delicious food on an extensive menu at reasonable prices.

Rino's has become somewhat more famous in recent days since Guy Fieri of the Food Network show *Diners, Drive-Ins, and Dives* visited this establishment and provided some extremely complimentary commentary along with crystal clear video of a special dinner preparation including the making of homemade pasta. Guy also interviewed the chef, Anthony, and it is clear that Anthony's enthusiasm for his work and his attention to detail make the restaurant successful.

I am often skeptical of television endorsements. It seems to me that a food critic's review or a movie critic's review is, more often than not, at odds with that which I have personally found to be true. This was not the case at Rino's. Guy Fieri's endorsement was 100 percent spot on, and the veracity of this endorsement leads me to believe that all of his episodes on *Diners, Drive-Ins, and Dives* are also 100 percent spot on.

It is critically important to build credibility in business and, sometimes, this takes longer than you may like. Trust or credibility needs to be earned through consistently honest communications. Guy Fieri proved his credibility with me tonight. We need to prove our credibility with others and know who to believe ourselves.

Chapter 34 | **Sandinistas & Lemonistas**

Do you remember the Sandinistas? In the early 1980s, this Nicaraguan political party joined with Cuba in supporting the growth of Marxism throughout Central and South America.

Marxism is an anti-capitalist, anti-American philosophy that purports to believe that there can and should be classless societies in the world that result in everyone being equal. Marxism believes that class differences create revolutions, and class differences are created when different people earn different amounts of income. This philosophy holds that, in spite of innate differences between and among humans, everyone is equal and everyone should be paid equally. There are no incentives for hard work or special talents. Marxists believe they have the answer for creating an ideal world, and capitalism, as practiced in the United States, is evil.

Have you ever heard of Lemonistas? Saturday, three people who looked to be clean-cut college-age students were arrested for selling lemonade at ten cents per cup on the west lawn of the Capitol building in Washington, D.C., without a permit. They were selling lemonade to protest recent lemonade stand shutdowns by police and health inspectors in different parts of the country. The Lemonistas, as they call themselves, are two women and a man. They helped to create "Lemonade Freedom Day," a new national day of protest against shutting down lemonade stands that do not have permits.

This morning I watched one woman Lemonista with the man who "created" or founded the group on national TV. The interviewer asked the founder, who seemed about twice the age of the Lemonista, what he hoped to achieve with the national attention now being provided to the Lemonistas. I was stunned when he said that he wanted "good people to disobey bad laws."

Although the Lemonistas portray themselves as just kids fighting for truth, justice, and the American way, their message of having "good people disobey bad laws" is actually a statement of anarchy. Anarchy is the absence of laws. If we followed the logic of the founder, different "good people" could disagree on what constitutes a "bad law" and, eventually, there could be no laws because someone would think every law is bad.

Now, it is not plausible to assume that these three kids are going to start a revolution, and I do not think anyone actually feels threatened by the Lemonistas. In fact, I think many people think the Lemonistas are "cute," they have a "cute" name, and, possibly, they did a good thing. I think this sentiment arises due to fond memories of lemonade stands from yesteryear. However, are sympathizers confusing image with reality?

There are reasons to stop unauthorized lemonade sales in today's society. Even young children can be used as pawns by the treacherous and deceitful to possibly harm the innocent. However, whether we agree with shutting down unauthorized lemonade stands or not, that is not the issue.

In business, words must be clearly understood and not hidden in a preconceived notion. If the notion were meant to be the communication and not the words, the notion would have been stated. In the case of the Lemonistas, the words are clear. The Lemonistas are, in some ways, espousing a similar philosophy to that of the Sandinistas of the 1980s; I wonder if any of them, including their founder, consciously took the name Lemonistas to sound like the Sandinistas. You have heard the expression, "Don't shoot the messenger." In the case of the Lemonistas and in cases like theirs, it may be more appropriate to say, "Don't miss the message."

Chapter 35

Earthquakes & Wake-Up Calls

Would you believe there are about five hundred thousand earthquakes each year? Would you believe there are about one million earthquakes each year? Well, from the best I can determine, the truth may be a number that is significantly greater than one million. So, when an earthquake hits, why are we so amazed or, even, frightened?

Almost all of the earthquakes on the globe cannot be felt by humans, and they are only picked up on seismometers. Seismometers measure an earthquake on the Richter scale. Generally, when a quake is less than 3, we cannot feel it. At around a 4 on the Richter scale, we can notice a quake; a 4 is ten times more powerful than a 3. A reading of 5, or moderate, is ten times more powerful than a 4. Each whole number on the Richter scale reflects a reading that is ten times more powerful than the previous whole number. Thus, the decimal point reading is a measure of earthquake force that is proportionately between two whole numbers.

Today, an earthquake with a Richter scale reading of 5.9 traveled up from Virginia through Boston and beyond. A reading of 5 to 6 or so on the Richter scale reflects a quake strong enough to possibly cause damage to buildings. A quake between 6 and 7 is quite serious, and over 7 is very dangerous – and these do not happen often. For example, the earthquake in Japan that occurred in March 2011 measured 8.9. This was a devastating earthquake. Quakes over 8 have historically occurred only once per year on a global basis.

Many people in Boston felt the earthquake today. There was a heightened level of anxiety by many who actually experienced shaking in their workplace buildings.

I did not personally feel the earthquake, but each of our children working in Boston did feel the quake. Since our children had some of their growing-up years in Salt Lake City, they were not very concerned. Salt Lake City is on the Wasatch fault—a major fault in North America—prone to earthquakes that could be felt by people. Therefore, our children always received earthquake preparedness training in their Salt Lake City school. However, the slight movement of buildings was certainly concerning to those individuals who did not ever think an earthquake would happen in Boston, where earthquakes are unheard of.

As a result of today's earthquake, some in Boston are saying that earthquake preparedness needs to be improved. Naturally, it should. Instead of having an earthquake of 5.9, we could have had one of 7.9. Then, without any serious earthquake awareness or preparedness among the citizens, our coping with devastation would be much harder than it otherwise could have been. Fortunately, we did not have an earthquake that was greater than 5.9, but that does not mean that we forget about awareness and preparation for the future. Today was a wake-up call.

In business, wake-up calls are not always so "moving" as today's earthquake, but they should not be left unanswered. There may not be a second chance at recovery from another similar event. Thus, we should take preparatory or preventive action immediately before the wake-up communication is forgotten and risk to the business returns. One easy example here happens to be a fairly obvious one. Specifically, when a business owner has a heart attack and returns to the business a couple of months later, shouldn't the business owner be thinking about whether another heart attack might occur? If this owner did not have a business continuity plan in place before the heart attack, he or she should certainly put one in place immediately after the heart attack.

| **Hurricane Irene & Addressing Problems At Their Core**

Hurricane Irene knocked out the communication lines in our Wellesley home last night, and we have not had home-based cable TV, Internet, or phone at any time today or tonight. Further, as it turns out, we are unable to determine when the communication lines may go up again because our service provider is not having calls to its service center answered by live voices. There is only a recording for residents of our zip code who call the company, which acknowledges that communications are down and the company is attempting to fix the problem.

What's wrong with this picture?

Hurricane Irene is only a category 1 hurricane, and it caused our home-based communication lines to be put out of commission. A category 1 hurricane is only slightly greater than a tropical storm. What if Irene had been a category 5, the strongest type of hurricane? Our significant problems from today's category 1 hurricane suggest to me that our communication infrastructure is not very well equipped to handle stress. Then, after thinking of all the local areas without both power and communications, like parts of the Cape, I began to think we need to examine our entire utility infrastructure. In short, I wondered why we can't do better. If the reason is that we have old technology supporting our daily lives, it seems to me that now is the time to update. In that regard, Irene has delivered a wake-up call. However, who will listen?

What's right with this picture?

Hurricane Irene provided Julie and me and tens of thousands of other individuals—who have not had severe damage—with a day almost free of emails, phone calls, and television. With our home computers, televisions, and phone lines down, we are forced to have a large portion of our day in conversation, book reading, reflection, or the like. Additionally, human interaction was almost brought back to its natural state of face-to-face dialogue. Within this context, it is both fortunate and unfortunate that iPhones and other mobile devices still worked today. It is fortunate, of course, in the event these devices could help in the time of an emergency. It is unfortunate that we could not have an entire day free from the electronic age.

So, I pondered the pros and the cons of this day without cable TV, Internet, and phone. Today could have been considered either a waste of a day or a day of unexpected opportunity. I determined the day was pleasant, productive, and a welcomed surprise. Would you have thought the same?

In business, a wake-up call—or a wake-up communication—can be misinterpreted or ignored. Hurricane

Irene exposed the extreme vulnerability of our home-based communication lines. Yet, it is not likely that the service provider will attempt a long-term, corrective strengthening of the communications system. So, the problem will occur again with another storm after the system is fixed in the near term. If this type of vulnerability were discovered in a non-utility type of business, the problem would probably be addressed at its core. It would be impractical to repeatedly address the same issue time and time again, consuming business resources, including time, money, and, possibly, customer goodwill. There may be some short-term benefits to not addressing the problem at its core, like an easy or cheap fix and, as in the case of the hurricane, more free time. However, short-term gain will be quickly lost in long-term pain by not fixing a problem right. Listen to wake-up calls; remember to recognize and address all problems at their core.

Chapter 37

Flash Flooding & Asking For Help

Our house in Wellesley faces north, and the front foundation of our house is slightly below street level on a downward sloping hill. Our driveway goes down a steep hill on the eastern side of our house and circles around the back to a two-car garage tucked under the house. Because our driveway slopes down, we have a catch basin for rain at the end of the driveway. The cover for the catch basin is about the size of a street manhole cover and it is about forty to forty-five feet away from the edge of the garage. It is also below the surface of the garage by about one foot due to the slope in the driveway. There is shrubbery behind the drain and across the back border of our driveway, which is on a narrow, slightly elevated strip of solid land.

We were beginning to feel the effects of Hurricane Irene in the late afternoon. Because Irene was only a category 1 hurricane, flooding from the storm was the major concern, not damage from the winds.

At about four o'clock, we experienced extremely heavy rains and flash flooding throughout the area. About this time, our driveway also began to experience a flash flood, and water was moving quickly up the driveway and toward the house. The water was forming a pool between the elevated strip of solid land behind the driveway and the edge of the garage. Fortunately, after about twenty minutes the rain lightened up and the water in the driveway receded before entering the garage. As this driveway flooding was happening, Julie and I began to quickly move as many of our possessions as possible off of the first floor of our house, which is on the garage level. At the same time, I placed a couple of calls to friends for any ideas whatsoever on how to combat the flash flooding occurring in our driveway.

Unbelievably, one friend got in his truck with his two daughters and went to a nearby farm, before it closed at five o'clock, to pick up ten bales of hay. He brought over the hay and some plastic, and we made a barrier in front of the garage. As the afternoon and evening progressed, flash flooding continued in the area and in our driveway. However, the water in our driveway never made it past the edge of the newly constructed barrier before it began to recede again.

We were fortunate on two scores today. First, due to our friend's creativity and quick action, we found a line of defense for the flash flooding with the hay barrier. Second, our friend was willing and able to help.

In business, many times we need help but are afraid or unwilling to ask. In fact, it is often easier to help someone than to ask for help. We should not be shy about asking for help; people often want to help—whether they are paid consultants or unpaid friends or family members—and almost always the business will benefit.

TEAMWORK

Teamwork is critical to the success of a business. Teamwork is required for the development and execution of plans, analyses, and messages. The right team members will create a strong plan with strong supporting analyses and strong messaging; this team will carry the excitement and enlightenment created by the achievement of these tasks into the marketplace with a level of enthusiasm that will increase the probability of success.

Virtually everyone works in a team of some sort. Whether it is a sole proprietor or a small business owner with four employees, these businesspeople have suppliers of office products, lead-generation groups, friends upon whom ideas are bounced, technology service providers for computers, phone, and the Internet, and more. A sole proprietor or a small business owner with four employees is not really alone—although it often feels that way. Think of sports. It is clear on the surface that professional football, baseball, soccer, basketball, and hockey are team sports. Professional tennis and golf are considered individual sports, but are they really? Tennis players have coaches, sponsors, and, often, family members to support them. Golfers have the same group as well as caddies with whom they can discuss the approach for every shot. Therefore, even an individual sport is not really an individual sport. Teamwork is essential for success.

The vignettes in this section are light, but effective, reminders from everyday living on the importance of having the proper team, and on how to celebrate and develop that team to make it stronger. Strong teams will make for a strong business.

Chapter 38

**The Brewster Flats
& Scallop Shells**

The Brewster Flats are tidal flats on Cape Cod Bay.

The Brewster Flats are phenomenal because a person can walk out over a mile into Cape Cod Bay during low tide on hard-packed sand. Occasionally, there are small pools of water along the one-mile route that usually get no deeper than mid-thigh on an average adult. These pools can be used for wading or, even, swimming. A person can also explore various types of sea life when the tides recede. For example, hermit crabs, eels, and clams are sometimes exposed. Additionally, sea gulls can be seen strutting on the wet sand before feasting on newly exposed marine life.

Brewster has eight beaches on Cape Cod Bay or the Brewster Flats. The beaches are delightful at high tide since the water is clear and usually much warmer than the ocean. Additionally, there are small waves, if any, making swimming, wading, or tossing a ball easy and refreshing—almost like being in a pond.

Julie and I went to Crosby Beach in Brewster today. We usually go to the Brewster beaches on Cape Cod Bay, and we occasionally go to the ocean at Nauset Beach in East Orleans. We usually take our lunch and bring two or three newspapers and a couple of magazines. We always have more than enough sunscreen lotion, and we use an umbrella to shade us over our beach chairs.

Today, Julie took an extended walk up and down the beach to collect shells. She likes to collect Atlantic Bay scallop shells. After walking for nearly an hour, Julie returned with a handful of nearly perfect Atlantic Bay scallop shells. These delicate shells are often about two inches in length and width. They have a fanlike molding along their semi-circular top and a box-like shape at the base. They can be gray, pink, salmon, purple, or lavender in color. They are quite beautiful to examine and display, and no two shells are exactly the same.

Julie has been collecting shells since she was a young child. She carefully scrutinizes each shell before she decides to keep it with her other shells in a round, glass bowl in our home. She periodically takes out her shells to admire and enjoy. In many ways, Julie's process of collecting shells reminds me of her careful process of selecting and keeping her friends. Whether from college or from our many moves around the country and Canada, Julie has made friends who have lasted a lifetime. Each friend is different but always there—regardless of wherever they move or we move. They are always there to be admired and enjoyed.

In business, we should look for teammates as carefully as Julie looks for scallop shells. Although this is not always practical to do, we need to be comfortable with colleagues in multiple areas, including integrity, respect, intelligence, and support. These qualities will help create a pleasant and challenging work environment that should result in positive business outcomes to problems and opportunities. If this type of workplace environment does not exist, it should be sought by both those doing the hiring and those being hired.

Chapter 39

**US Women's Soccer
Team & Goals**

This year, FIFA became 107 years old. FIFA is the international governing body for soccer, commonly called football in other countries around the world. FIFA stands for Federation Internationale de Football Association, and it is headquartered in Zurich, Switzerland. FIFA was formed when representatives from seven countries, France, Belgium, Denmark, Netherlands, Spain, Sweden, and Switzerland, signed an agreement in Paris on May 21, 1904. FIFA sponsors the World Cup, the world's Super Bowl of soccer.

Today, the US women's World Cup soccer team lost the World Cup's championship game in a heartbreaker to the women of Japan in a shootout. A shootout means overtime finished in a tie, and the next way to resolve the battle is to have five players from each team take alternating penalty shots to determine which team will win. Unfortunately, we lost despite a valiant effort.

The US women's World Cup soccer players are hardworking, dedicated individuals who represented their country with pride and respect in games of importance from a global perspective.

In business as in World Cup soccer, teams operate best with clear goals. With the US women's soccer team, the goal was to win the World Cup. With many businesses, the goal is to become the leader in their product or service categories or in their geographic markets. Thus, even if a business does not reach the goal, like the US women's soccer team, a finish near the goal can often still result in success and pride. Goals can also be less lofty, but equally challenging, like an objective of a 10 percent increase in sales. However, a business without goals is a business without a purpose or mission. Without goals, the chance of success for a team is minimized.

Chapter 40

Abbey Road & Come Together

The last album recorded by The Beatles was *Abbey Road*, released in 1969. Of note, the last album released by The Beatles—but recorded earlier than *Abbey Road*—was *Let It Be* in 1970. I think *Abbey Road* is a great album, and I am not alone. In 1992, *Rolling Stone Magazine* placed it number fourteen in the top five hundred albums of all time. The lead song on *Abbey Road* is "Come Together."

There are different interpretations of the song "Come Together," including one that says each verse is a description of one of The Beatles. For example, the phrase, "He got joo-joo eyeball, he one holy roller," could be a reference to George since he was into his religious pursuits at that time. "He got Ono sideboard, he one spinal cracker" could refer to John and Yoko Ono. "Got to be good-looking cos he's so hard to see," could refer to Paul, the handsome Beatle. "He got monkey finger, he shoot Coca-Cola," could refer to Ringo's known and public drinking of Coca-Cola.

"Come Together" could be interpreted as describing a team—with each member having different characteristics and qualities—even though The Beatles were then on the verge of breaking up.

I found and bought a wall hanging for my office today, a fully displayed original *Abbey Road* album jacket with a partially displayed original *Abbey Road* vinyl record matted inside a beautiful frame.

I am going to hang the *Abbey Road* wall hanging in my office because it will be a reminder to me and to all who come into my office that, in business, we need to come together, as a team, to reach our goals. Additionally, it is to the advantage of the business that we have team members with different characteristics and qualities because that only adds to the strength of the team.

Chapter 41

**Hitting Streaks
& The Company We Keep**

A hitting streak is a baseball term for the number of consecutive games in which a player gets at least one base hit. However, contrary to popular opinion, there are times when a baseball player can be at bat during a game without a hit and keep a hitting streak alive. According to official baseball rules, a streak is not ended when a player does not get a hit in a game due to being hit by a pitch, reaching base on a defensive interference call such as hitting the catcher's mitt on a swing, or executing a sacrifice bunt. The streak would end on a sacrifice fly, however.

Joe DiMaggio holds the Major League Baseball record for a hitting streak. He hit in fifty-six consecutive games in 1941 as a New York Yankee.

There are over fifty names listed in baseball history with hitting streaks of thirty or more games. Joe DiMaggio holds the Major League record and the American League record. Willie Keeler is second on an all-time basis and holds the National League record at forty-five games, playing for Baltimore in 1896-1897 when it was a National League team. Pete Rose is third all-time with a forty-four game streak in 1978 when he played for the Cincinnati Reds in the National League. Three American League players who have been inducted into the Baseball Hall of Fame are the only hitters listed twice, Ty Cobb of the Detroit Tigers in 1911 and 1917, George Sisler of the St. Louis Browns in 1922 and 1924-25, and Sam Rice of the Washington Senators in 1924 and 1929-30. There are over fifteen players who are tied with thirty-game hitting streaks.

The Boston baseball teams have five names on the list of players with hitting streaks of thirty or more games. Two are from the National League's Boston Braves, who became the Milwaukee Braves in 1953 and then the Atlanta Braves in 1966. Three are from the American League's Boston Red Sox:

1. Tommy Holmes is number nine on the list with a hitting streak of thirty-seven consecutive games in 1945 when he played for the Boston Braves. Tommy Holmes was runner-up for the National League's Most Valuable Player (MVP) award that year with a .352 batting average and League leading totals in hits (224), home runs (28), and doubles (47).

2. Dom DiMaggio is tied with two other players for number sixteen on the list with a hitting streak of thirty-four consecutive games in 1949 when he played for the Red Sox. In 1949, Dom DiMaggio hit .307 with 126 runs. Ironically, his streak was ended on August 9 by an outstanding catch made by his brother Joe of the New York Yankees.

3. Tris Speaker is tied on the list with a hitting streak of thirty consecutive games in 1912 when he played for the Red Sox. He played in almost every game that year and led the American League in doubles (53) and home runs (10). He had a .383 batting average and led the Red Sox to the World Series title that year, over the New York Giants.

4. Lance Richbourg is also tied on the list with a hitting streak of thirty consecutive games over two seasons, 1927 and 1928, when he played for the Boston Braves. In 1927, Richbourg had a .309 batting average, and in 1928 he had a .337 batting average.

5. Nomar Garciaparra is also tied on the list with a hitting streak of thirty consecutive games in 1997 when he played for the Red Sox and was named American League Rookie of the Year. He hit thirty home runs with ninety-eight RBIs and a .306 batting average in 1997. He also set a new Major League record for RBIs by a leadoff hitter and most home runs by a rookie shortstop.

Dustin Pedroia is the current second baseman for the Boston Red Sox. Tonight, he hit in his twenty-third consecutive game. What is almost more impressive is that he was hitting "clean-up," or fourth, in the mighty Red Sox lineup tonight. Pedroia is listed as five feet nine inches tall and 180 pounds, but I doubt he's that big. Yet, he batted clean-up tonight, a slot usually reserved for large, powerful men who can, theoretically, be counted on for hitting home runs.

If Pedroia does reach a thirty-game hitting streak, he will be in the company of some great baseball players who span the history of the game. Pedroia does not have a choice in the company of people he will join if he reaches the record books with a thirty-game hitting streak. However, just by reaching a thirty-game hitting streak, some people will consider him among the elite players to have ever played the game.

In business, we have a choice in the company of people we keep. When we choose a company, that is the first step in that process. A second step is who we associate with in our day-to-day work tasks. A third step is who, from work, we choose to be with during our "free time at the office" or after hours. Through our colleague associations, others will form opinions on our character, knowledge, professionalism, and more. Therefore, it is important to be careful about the company we keep, and how we keep it, for reputational purposes.

Chapter 42

Job Stress & The Hootchies

There are many books, articles, and surveys about job stress at work. The topic is a major area of study for both government agencies and private enterprise. Here is just one research finding: the American Psychological Association, or APA, the largest association of psychologists in the world, found that three-quarters of Americans feel that work has a significant impact on stress levels. I'm sure this is no surprise to you.

Julie and I tried a local bar with live music tonight called The Woodshed at the request of our son, Michael. The Woodshed is an old barn in Brewster that has two bars, tables, and a place for a band to setup and play. Apparently, it is very well known in the area. Julie and I always thought it was a place for young people, but now we know people of all ages go there.

We arrived at The Woodshed before the band began to set up. The band was called The Hootchies.

When The Hootchies began to set up, all four members appeared to enjoy the process and seemed to be looking forward to playing that evening. The musicians included a drummer, a keyboard player, a lead guitar, and a bass guitar. We were sitting at a table directly in front of a very small stage.

The Hootchies were good; I would see them again. They played songs that they called Northern Fried Rock. In short, they played music that was familiar to Julie and me as well as to Michael and his girlfriend, who were with us.

It seemed The Hootchies have day jobs, but it is clear that they love their evening and weekend music gigs.

Given the stress levels in business, it is important to have outlets for stress relief. The Hootchies have this outlet in their music. Others have it in sports or family activities. Whatever the outlet, stress relief activities should be encouraged and supported in order to help create a more pleasant and a more stable workplace.

Chapter 43 | **Sixtieth Birthday & Memorable Events**

Tonight, Julie, our friends, Mark Jurilla, who works with me, and his wife, Jillian, and all of our family members and several other friends surprised me with a party for my sixtieth birthday, about a week before my actual birthday. There were about forty people present at the party, including our daughter, Beth, and her husband, Adam, our son, Michael, and his girlfriend, and our daughter, Cortney.

The party was held at the upstairs at Tartufo restaurant in Newton Centre, Massachusetts. Renovations at Tartufo had just been completed on Saturday, two days prior to the party. Our party was the first event in the newly renovated upstairs.

As I walked up the stairs to a private dining area, there was dead silence. Then, as I emerged from the staircase to see the waiting group of friends and family, I heard a chorus of "Happy Birthday" and "Surprise!" It was a great start to a great evening.

I have never been one to put too much emphasis on birthdays. Of course, Julie and I would always celebrate birthdays for our children and for each other, but we never went overboard. I have always thought birthdays were gifts; they were not earned. Therefore, I would rather put extra effort into an "earned" celebration such as a promotion at work or a move to a new home rather than a birthday. However, tonight I realized something new.

A birthday is a gift, and so is a party. Tonight's party created a gift of a memory that I will always keep…and so will my family. We will talk about it periodically for the rest of my life. For me, from now on, a birthday is a gift, a party is a gift, and a happy memory may be the greatest gift of all.

In business, we need to create happy, memorable events, too. This will allow all team members to talk about these events over the years and build history around them. Then, when times get tough, there is always a happy remembrance to help offset the short-term pain.

Chapter 44

**Max & His College
Baseball Coach**

The Cape Cod Baseball League began the playoffs
tonight with eight teams vying for the championship:
four in the Eastern Division and four in the Western
Division. It is a big night for baseball on Cape Cod, and
thousands of spectators attend each playoff game. In all,
there were four games tonight. The Harwich Mariners
and the Orleans Firebirds were the home teams in the
East, and the Falmouth Commodores and the Bourne
Braves were the home teams in the West. Julie and I
attended the Harwich game because the Mariners were
hosting the Brewster Whitecaps, our team.

The Brewster-Harwich game tonight was a classic
pitchers' duel, won by the Whitecaps 3-1.

Julie and I were sitting in the grandstands between
home plate and first base, which represented the Brewster side of the field. I was sitting on the end of the fifth
row on the first-base side of the stands. There were people standing to my right in a space between our seats and
a much larger seating area or grandstand that started
about twenty feet to my right and continued down the
right field line.

In the eighth inning, a new pitcher for Brewster entered the game: Max Garner from Austin, Texas, and Baylor University. On one of his first pitches, I yelled loudly from my end seat something like, "What a pitch!" "Was that a slow curve?" It was a great pitch that caused the batter to swing and miss by a wide margin, but I don't think anyone could have hit that pitch. Then, the man standing to my right in the crowded open area between the two sets of bleacher-like seats said to me, "That was a curve with a drop." I said, "What a drop!"

Having played and coached baseball and having been a baseball dad myself, I thought I recognized a little too much surety in the response from the man next to me to suggest that he was a normal spectator. Therefore, I decided to ask a conversational question or two while we admired the pitches of Max.

First, I asked the man if he was rooting for Brewster or Harwich. He answered, "Brewster." Then, having clearly heard his Texas accent, I asked whether he was related to anyone on the team. He said he was the pitcher's dad. As we continued in our conversation, he volunteered that he had taught Max the pitch that I thought was magnificent: an overhand curve with a drop. He also said that when the pitch is working, like it was tonight, it is terrific.

Julie and I congratulated this father, Steve Garner, on having a son in the Cape Cod Baseball League. He was appreciative of the recognition and said that it had been quite a struggle for his son to get here.

His son, Max, was listed on the roster tonight as 6'3" and 195 pounds. However, not too long ago, his dad said he was about forty-five pounds lighter.

Following Max's freshman year at Baylor, Steve said his son developed severe ulcerative colitis. This is a disease that causes inflammation and ulcers in the lining of the colon. As a result, fatigue and weight loss occur, as well as excruciating pain. His son dropped to about 150 pounds and had to withdraw from school. He had to stay home with his family for treatment and recovery during what otherwise would have been his sophomore year at Baylor.

As we continued speaking about Max, Steve said the Baylor coach, Steve Smith, was terrific during the entire difficult and painful period of his son's saga from diagnosis to recovery. Steve said the coach never wavered in his complete support of his son and the coach would not even consider removing his scholarship—even when his son's condition was at its worst, which could have been life threatening. The coach wanted to do everything possible to help pull Max through this very terrible ordeal both mentally and physically. I was somewhat stunned by this compassionate baseball story in the midst of a cutthroat collegiate sports world where scholarships are routinely given and routinely taken away, but I said that I had always heard Baylor was a good school and this wholehearted support by the Baylor coach is consistent with what I know of Baylor's fine reputation.

Steve said that his son, at first, did not want to speak about his medical situation with anyone as he returned to play baseball after a remarkable recovery. However, as Max traveled around the college baseball circuit last season, stories starting appearing in college newspapers and the general press about Max. So, in fact, Steve said Max's story was no longer confidential. It is now a public human-interest story.

Max pitched the eighth inning and struck out two batters. He did not allow a run, and he looked great.

In business, it is important to support team members—even when things are tough. This type of support takes the fear out of the workplace for many workers while fostering an environment of success over the long term. Just as Max had a comeback, there are many stories of individuals having comebacks in business, too. We just need to be aware and supportive of team members during difficult periods.

Today is August 9. There were many famous historical events that took place on this day in history, in addition to my birthday. For example, here are a dozen that come to my mind:

1. In 1809, William Barret Travis was born in South Carolina. Travis was the commander of a small band of volunteer troops, including Davy Crockett, one of my historical heroes, and Jim Bowie, who fought the battle of the Alamo in San Antonio, Texas, in 1836 in an effort to have Texas gain independence from Mexico.

2. In 1930, the cartoon character Betty Boop was introduced to the world in Max Fleisher's animated cartoon called Dizzy Dishes.

3. In 1936, Jesse Owens won his fourth gold medal at the Berlin Olympics.

4. In 1938, Rod Laver was born. He was an Australian tennis champion who won the Grand Slam twice and was rated the world's number one player for seven consecutive years from 1964 to 1970.

5. In 1944, the character Smokey Bear debuted to educate the public about the danger of forest fires. Smokey said, "Remember, only YOU can prevent forest fires."

6. In 1945, the U.S. dropped the second atomic bomb on Japan in Nagasaki. This bomb led to Japan's surrender to the Allied Forces in World War II on August 15, 1945. The first atomic bomb was dropped on Hiroshima three days earlier.

7. In 1963, Whitney Houston was born in Newark, New Jersey. She is an award-winning singer and an actress.

8. In 1974, Richard Nixon resigned as president of the United States, and Gerald Ford became the thirty-eighth president.

9. In 1975, the first NFL game in the New Orleans Superdome was played. Houston beat New Orleans 13-7 in a preseason game with 72,434 people in attendance.

10. In 1988, the Chicago Cubs beat the New York Mets in the first official Major League Baseball night game at Chicago's Wrigley Field.

11. Also in 1988, the Edmonton Oilers of the National Hockey League traded Wayne Gretzky to the Los Angeles Kings.

12. In 1995, Jerry Garcia of the Grateful Dead died.

I remember specific historical events that took place on my birthday. I could have easily made a list of twenty or more events and elaborated to the tune of two or three paragraphs on each. However, for illustrative purposes, the list above works.

In business, we need to make lists. Teams need priorities, sales champions need to be found and crowned, customers need to be ranked in terms of importance, and more. A list is a simple way of communicating to a team a statement of importance without any commentary. The facts speak for themselves. Lists can be very effective if not overdone or overwhelming. They can spur performance by some and demoralize others. Use them carefully.

Chapter 46 | **The Pats & Rational, Confident Behavior**

Sports championships are important to the psyche of regions, and the area around Boston has certainly had its share of championships in recent years. In fact, Boston is now called the City of Champions. This is because in the last seven years, Boston teams have won the football Super Bowl with the New England Patriots in 2004 (also 2001 and 2003), the baseball World Series with the Red Sox in 2007 (and 2004), the National Basketball Association championship with the Boston Celtics in 2008, and now the hockey Stanley Cup with the Bruins in 2011.

It is ironic to me that the Boston team that is considered the strongest, year in and year out, the New England Patriots, is now the team farthest removed from a championship.

The Patriots played their first preseason game last night after having little time for practice since the National Football League labor dispute ended a couple of weeks ago. They massacred the visiting Jacksonville Jaguars, 47-12, but scores don't count in preseason. This is because stars and other starting players do not play very much, if at all, in preseason games for fear of risking an injury before the regular season begins. Within this usual context, Tom Brady, the star quarterback for the Patriots, did not even play last night, and neither did the recently acquired "big name" receiver, Chad Ochocinco, who was delivered from the Cincinnati Bengals.

So, as you can imagine, a 47-12 win by the Patriots, without Brady or Ochocinco or star receiver Wes Welker playing even one minute, stirs visions of another Super Bowl win for the Pats. Thus, the expectations for the season have been set: a Super Bowl win.

What happens with lofty expectations? In business, the common catchphrase for setting expectations is "under-promise and over-deliver." This way, everyone is happy when the work is complete. How can a sports team as strong as the Patriots under-promise and over-deliver, having already won three Super Bowls in the last ten years and having massacred the Jaguars last night without Brady and some others having playing time? The answer is they can't, but they can talk about the unpredictability of the game, the comparability of talent among the stronger teams, and the respect they have for other players in the league. In other words, they can act with class and confidence without promising a Super Bowl win. They are, in effect, promising their best efforts and, if they don't win a Super Bowl, it won't be for lack of trying; this modest and rational approach permeates the organization from the ownership to the last player on the roster.

The Pats, as well as The New York Football Giants, and some other professional football teams epitomize the best in professional sports—a rational level of confidence, a steady approach to winning and losing, and a "best efforts" display on the field and in the front office. Fans appreciate this approach and its lasting effects on the game, and this approach often translates to the fan base in the region as it has in Boston.

In our businesses, we also need our teams—from the top to the bottom—to display a rational level of confidence, a steady approach to the business, and best efforts always. This will help foster a team that desires to win in the marketplace over the long term, while understanding there will always be setbacks in the near term. Often, this type of behavior needs to start at the top. However, this behavior can start anywhere in an organization and spread, but, eventually, it must be supported by the top if it did not start there.

Chapter 47

Work Van & Company Reputation

Route 9 is an east-west road that travels across the entire state of Massachusetts. Like the Massachusetts Turnpike, it runs from Boston to the western border of the state. Unlike the Massachusetts Turnpike, it has traffic lights, businesses, and homes along the route. It also has fewer lanes and, generally, a lower speed limit.

I have two preferred routes for getting to work each morning in Newton, and one route includes a small stretch of Route 9 between Wellesley and Newton, a city just east of Wellesley and just west of Boston.

I was stopped in the right lane of Route 9 east this morning in a line of vehicles behind a traffic light. I was directly behind a work van for a relatively well-known window replacement company located in the Boston area. The van had two ladders on its roof and the company name, logo, and phone number on the back doors.

All of a sudden, I saw a big, crumpled breakfast bag from a fast food restaurant thrown out the passenger window. I was angry. We generally have very clean roads and streets in our area, and the residents of Newton and Wellesley are very proud of their communities in several ways, including cleanliness. This was clearly an out-of-pattern occurrence that made me angry, and I assumed the workers in the truck did not come from Newton or Wellesley, but only did work there.

Since I was stopped in traffic, angry with the disrespectful trashing, and had the phone number of the company staring me in the face on the back door of the van, I called the store to register anger and seek corrective action for the future. I asked to speak to the owner, and, it turned out, the owner answered the phone.

In a brief summary, I told the owner of the window replacement company of the incident and that he should speak to the people in the van to see if they would own up to this incident and to tell them never to do this again. I also said I would tell my friends of this incident so that they would think twice before using this company. I provided the owner with the license plate of the vehicle, which was right in front of my nose. The owner said he appreciated my comments, but I could tell that he was shocked at receiving a call like this.

In business, all team member actions reflect on the business. Whether these actions are in vans, in the office, in the store, or online with activities such as Facebook, team members need to understand the impact and ramifications of their actions with regard to company reputation. If this is not intuitively obvious to all members of a team, then formal communications should be established to outline acceptable and unacceptable behavior while still respecting the individual rights of all team members. This is a critically important company activity, outside help with this project from lawyers or consultants may be helpful.

| **Special Places
& Optimum Performance**

Julie and I plan to leave Brewster and return to Wellesley early tomorrow morning to "batten down the hatches" before Hurricane Irene is scheduled to arrive. Preparations for the expected arrival of Irene is along the same lines as those that we took today in Brewster. For example, we need to put away deck furniture as well as the grill and hoses.

Before Hurricane Irene became a threat to our area, we had made plans to have cocktails and dinner with two couples tonight at the well-known and highly rated Chillingsworth restaurant in Brewster. After some phone and email discussions, we decided to keep our plans, despite the pending storm. However, one couple had family time pressures and could not stay for dinner. The couple that could not stay for dinner recently purchased a second home in Brewster, not too far from our house.

The couple with the Brewster home was spending their first full summer on the Cape. Previously, they had only gone to the Cape for a couple of weeks of vacation in the summer and for long summer week-ends. This year's full summer experience was new to them.

All six of us discussed the many things to do in Brewster, from bike riding on the Cape Cod Rail Trail to watching the Cape Cod Baseball League. We all agreed that Brewster had great restaurants, too. However, this new-to-Brewster couple was finding it a little odd to be on the Cape the entire summer.

It did not seem quite natural yet to the new Brewster couple that they did not need to return to the Boston area to "batten down the hatches" as Julie and I were going to do and as the other couple was going to do. This new Brewster couple was planning to ride out the storm on the Cape because their Boston area home was already closed up for the summer. Therefore, they didn't have to do anything extra to prepare for a possible hurricane.

The new Brewster couple also said that they did not find it totally comfortable yet to be conducting all their work from their Brewster home this summer. The Cape had always been a special place for them and now work and their "special place" were in the same house; they had not yet figured out how to keep the Cape special while working from their home at the Cape.

In today's electronic 24/7 stressful world, it is not strange to have business follow us around. However, it is important to ensure that we have a place to go that allows us to clear our minds and refresh from business. This recharging—whether it is done in a TV room, a special place, or at a regularly scheduled time—is important for team members and for the team, as a whole, to maintain optimum performance. When we invite work into our special areas of space or time, we will have difficulty reenergizing, and, over time, we will need to be careful that work does not wear us down, resulting in less than optimum performance.

Fantasy Football is an online football game played by tens of millions of people around the country. I have seen estimates that put the enrollment in this game each season at about 10 percent of the US population, or about 30 million people.

Fantasy Football is great fun and, at its core, it allows people to act as owners or coaches of their own football teams during each week of the regular NFL season. Before each season, game participants choose individual National Football League players in a draft to fill their team rosters, including offensive scoring players who are quarterbacks, running backs, wide receivers, tight ends, and kickers. They also choose a defensive team, and individual defensive players can be chosen as well. Points for a person's team are awarded on how well their individual players do each week. For example, points are awarded on the offense for touchdowns, running yards, receiving yards, field goals, and extra points, and on the defense for quarterback sacks, interceptions, and points allowed.

Fantasy Football increases the knowledge of the game of football for fans. This is because each week, people playing Fantasy Football need to adjust their rosters to accommodate the individual strengths and weaknesses of their roster players while considering the opponents of each of their players as well. Fans get to examine and, if they wish, study football statistics.

The players on each person's fantasy team are from many different NFL teams. This is because all NFL players are available for drafting, and there are usually eight to twelve teams in a fantasy league. The drafting of players takes place—one pick at a time—until team rosters are filled. As a result of the draft, the best players in the NFL are usually chosen first, and the best players come from many different teams.

Since fantasy roster players come from several different teams, conflicts for fantasy team owners often occur when they watch an actual NFL game. They may be rooting for their favorite teams to win each week, but if a fantasy roster player is on an opposing team, the fan wants that player to do well, too. This conflict is fun to watch and makes for great conversations each week among fans.

I have been playing Fantasy Football for more years than I care to count. I began playing with only one team per year. In more recent years, I have had two or three teams each year.

Fantasy Football does not take much time to play each week as long as NFL game watching is not considered part of the game! Weekly team preparation can take as little as a few minutes or as much as a couple of hours. However, the weekly enjoyment coming from participating in this game is only limited by the number of hours in a week.

Tonight, I participated in a league draft for one of my teams for this year. Drafts are usually one of three types. First, there can be live draft at someone's house or a restaurant with all team owners present and one person writing draft selections on a large white board, with each selection needing to be made within a time limit. Second, drafts can also be live online, where draft choices can be made from a computer with each team owner participating, still with a time limit on each selection. Third, drafts for teams can be computer selected based on the preferences of the team owners, but without team owners present. This method is especially useful for accommodating team owners who are from different states with busy schedules.

I have participated in all three types of drafts over the years and I enjoy them all. It is always relatively easy to adjust team rosters as the season progresses if a player is not doing well or gets injured.

Overall, I think Fantasy Football relieves everyday business stress for owners of teams by making each week of the season more fun.

In business, I believe finding areas of fun and stress relief are important. Fantasy Football works for me. Playing musical instruments may work for you. If neither works for you, there are a myriad of other avocations, and, assuming no avocation presents a distraction from work but only an enhancement to the energy of the business team, it should be encouraged.

Chapter 50

The Internet & Job Creation

Joseph Carl Robnett Licklider was born in 1915 in St. Louis, Missouri, and died in 1990 in Arlington, Massachusetts. During his professional career, he was appointed to head the Information Processing Techniques Office at the US Advanced Research Projects Agency (ARPA). He led a group of researchers and scientists in this position. In the early 1960s, he envisioned a computer system that would share information. His vision led to his team's development of ARPANet, the precursor to the Internet. As such, he can be called the founder of the Internet—along with his team members, of course.

It is easy to understand how the Internet, itself, has changed the lives of everyone on this planet. However, I have found that people often forget that the Internet created an entirely new industry, including new jobs with completely new job descriptions.

There are many millions of people in the Internet industry around the world. For example, with the Internet virtually ubiquitous, we can now argue that all of Microsoft's nearly ninety thousand employees are in the Internet space. We can do the same for Intel's over eighty thousand employees and Apple's nearly fifty thousand employees. We can even argue that mobile phone companies have Internet-related jobs, including Nokia with over one hundred thousand employees and Verizon with over eighty thousand employees.

Additionally, it is indisputable that all of Google's nearly thirty thousand employees, all of eBay's nearly twenty thousand employees, and all of Yahoo!'s approximately thirteen thousand employees are in the Internet industry. It is impossible to count the total number of pure Internet small businesses that have been created. These Internet businesses are in every line of commerce, from companies that secure domain names like GoDaddy and Network Solutions to those that provide various forms of information like Carfax for used car information and Priceline for travel information and sales...and those are only US-created companies! Further, it is impossible to count the number of traditional businesses that now employ large numbers of individuals to handle their online information and sales channels, from Nordstrom to Bank of America.

As a result of the enormous size of the Internet industry, I should not be surprised that two of our children are in the Internet industry, Michael and Cortney.

I was speaking with Cortney today about her work in the Internet industry, and we were commenting on the state of the Internet industry as a whole. During our conversation, it occurred to me that within the Internet industry, the government and the private enterprise sectors inadvertently teamed up to create jobs through the development and use of the Internet. The government created it; the ingenuity and perseverance of private enterprise found commercial uses for it.

Joseph Carl Robnett Licklider and his team may have thought they were creating a communication tool, but they were really creating a jobs tool, too, through an unknowing or unacknowledged alliance with private enterprise. Sometimes, teams form naturally or result naturally from our efforts.

EPILOGUE

As you can see from reading this book, everyday living and the process of gaining business knowledge are greatly intertwined.

I hope it is now easy for you to recall the key processes for business by using the pneumonic device established in the title of this book: *The Business PACT*. Additionally, I hope you are now able to experience and create your own vignettes each day and discuss them with the people close to you on a periodic basis. The creation of your vignettes should provide great conversation, and, I believe, you will benefit at work by having a much clearer perspective on your business environment.

As you think about the vignettes in this book and your own, as you experience and create them, you will sometimes encounter difficulties classifying them into only one of the four key processes for business:

- Planning
- Analysis
- Communication
- Teamwork

I had difficulty classifying some of the vignettes in this book into only one category. For example, I categorized the chapter, "Bank of New York Mellon & Interest Rates," in *Planning* when I could have taken this story in a different direction and placed it into *Analysis*. I could have highlighted the thought behind the Bank of New York Mellon move and stopped there. However, the end point of this story is to plan for the future, therefore it fits into *Planning*. Additionally, the chapter, "The Cape Cod Rail Trail & The Bike Pump," is in Planning, but it just as easily could have been taken in a different direction and placed in *Teamwork*, emphasizing the need to support team members.

I believe that you, too, will sometimes have difficulty placing your vignettes into only one of the four categories. However, when you see or create a vignette that has two possible routes of learning or categorization, embrace both routes. Take a dual lesson. Share your ideas with others. Business is both an art and a science. There is not always one right answer.

Learn from the practicality in this book. Use this book as a guideline for better business performance. Use this book to better understand business tasks that need to be performed. Use this book to develop better business thinking.

Reread this book from time to time and refresh yourself with the basics of *The Business PACT*.

Made in the USA
Middletown, DE
31 August 2016